HOW TO MAKE

A MONSTER

AND WHY NO ONE CARES

A SENSIBLE LOOK AT RAMPAGE KILLERS

By Paul Glasco

To my friends, Donna and Paul!

Paul [signature]

2X

HOW TO MAKE A MONSTER
Copyright © 2021 by Paul Glasco
Third Edition

Written by Paul Glasco
Editing assistance by Greg Askew & Laura Evans
Cover art by Anthony Monceaux

ISBN 978-1-7377352-0-5 (softcover)
978-1-7377352-1-2 (hardcover)

Printed with pride in the United States of America.

For Holly — the definition of grace and class.

For Evan — the bright center of our universe.

Table of Contents

INTRODUCTION

It's safe to say that the majority of all broadcast, print, and online media work in lockstep with the many well-funded, anti-gun organizations in the United States. These two groups have shared the same left-leaning political views and disdain for the Second Amendment for as long as I can remember. Manufacturing and spreading misinformation about firearms and the firearm industry has also become big business in the U.S. Failed Presidential candidate, Michael Bloomberg, donated $38 million of his own money as part of Everytown for Gun Safety's combined $106 million annual cash haul in 2018.[1] And that's just *one* of the many well funded anti-gun groups that operate in America. With that kind of influence, it's no surprise that the messaging and nomenclature used to discuss and report on any topic that involves a firearm is purposely misleading — disingenuous at best.

So when the paid-for media reports on a murder of multiple people by a single killer who happens to choose a firearm to end people's lives, it's common and accepted now to use the phrase "mass shooting" and "mass shooter" when describing it. This choice of words is not accidental or by chance. This choice of words is meant to attach just as much negative press and stigma to the item chosen by the killer to kill as it does to the killer himself. And many times people are quicker to ask what kind of gun was used or how it was acquired rather than who the killer is and why he did it. This is a huge victory for the propaganda arm of the *anti-gun enterprise.*

That's right, I call it the "anti-gun enterprise" because the anti-gun movement is a very popular and lucrative business to be in. It is a big time industry — an enterprise. That $106 million dollars that Everytown raked in in 2018 went to paying massive salaries, printing t-shirts and signs, and funding travel to places all over the country to lobby against the Second Amendment. If you're wondering how that stacks up against other businesses, the average business in the United States has earnings of $4.9 million per year.[2] Wow! If I wasn't a principled person I'd consider starting an anti-gun organization myself!

To be clear, the anti-gun enterprise does a fabulous job of fund-raising, chanting slogans that rhyme, and printing t-shirts and signs. But all that money and all those efforts cannot, will not, and have never had any kind of affect on reducing the amount of rampage killers who choose guns to carry out their crimes. They speak of reducing "gun violence", but make no effort to actually do it.

But what are the pro-Second Amendment people doing to reduce "gun violence"? Well, they have their hands full fighting off the anti-gun enterprise's efforts, that's for sure. They also commit a ton of resources to firearm education programs as well as true gun safety initiatives. For example, the National Shooting Sports Foundation's Project Childsafe program partners with more than 15,000 law enforcement agencies and community partners across the country to distribute free firearm safety kits that include gun locks for safe firearm storage. This helps to contribute to the more than 100 million locking devices provided by the firearm industry to gun owners, free of charge.[3] This is what real "gun safety" looks like!

But if the anti-gun enterprise is committing their resources to restricting Second Amendment rights and the pro-gun organizations are committing their resources to promoting Second Amendment rights, who's trying to determine how we reduce the desire for humans to take the lives of other humans?

I WILL IF NO ONE ELSE WILL

Back in the 90's and early 2000's I worked for a Fortune 500 company and was in charge of hundreds of field employees as well as billing-related staff. While 90% of our upper management meetings and workshops were a complete waste of time, there were some that I learned from. One particular concept that was genius was equally simple — when faced with a problem, determine the root cause of it.

This book is in no way attempting to remove accountability for the heinous crimes against humanity that the subjects of these killings have committed. I come from a very strict upbringing where we all are to be held accountable for our own actions. If there was one decision I made along the way in life that could have prevented a serious issue and I chose wrong, that's on *me*. The goal with my book is to point out the things that we as brothers and sisters of our fellow man can look out for and possibly help future potential subjects and victims.

But we as gun rights advocates are constantly mocked by the anti-gun enterprise when we pray for murder victims as if our "thoughts and prayers" are somehow superficial. Supposedly, in their eyes, we don't care because we aren't willing to ban inanimate objects when a madman makes a conscious effort to kill other people. Yet the enterprise hijacks the phrase "gun safety" while teaching and promoting absolutely *zero* gun safety while simply trying to limit constitutional rights and banning guns. Where are their efforts to accurately identify the trigger of rampage killings? What research have they done to figure out what causes humans to initiate these events? Do they even care?

I care. And that's why I've written this book.

CHAPTER 1: THE MIND OF THE RAMPAGE KILLER

The FBI doesn't define "mass shooting" as a specific term. But it does define a "mass murderer" as someone who kills four or more people in one location and it doesn't necessarily have to be with a firearm. Although there is no official definition, it does seem as though the most commonly used definition of a *mass shooting* is as a single incident in which four or more people are shot or killed.[4] Harvard professor David Hemenway once said, "So there is no accepted definition of a 'mass shooting'…there are many, many different definitions of what a mass shooting is."[5] Clearly political party, business model, and ideology are the biggest reason why there isn't a common word for unspeakable crimes like this. And by various groups using different, yet accepted definitions for individuals who attack large groups of people, everyone pretty much has an excuse to deliver bad information since none of the definitions are universally agreed-upon or used. So, everyone else is right and everyone else is wrong depending on who's doing the reporting.

While much is made of mass shootings in today's world of immediately available news, they are actually very rare and only account for .05% of firearm-related deaths per year in the United States.[6] I know, judging by the amount of attention these events receive from the media and

politicians, you'd think it was an whirlwind epidemic —
but it's not.

So why aren't other attacks and murders reported by the
media and by politicians identified by the item the
perpetrators used to attack their victims with? When there's
a murder with a knife (1,591 in 2017), why don't they call
it a "knife death"? When a person drives into a crowd of
people with a moving truck (979 "other" in 2017), why
don't they call it a "mass run-over"? I think we can all
agree that firearms are a uniquely polarizing topic and any
negative press the media and politicians can generate
surrounding them is a small victory they can claim. By
employing classic *Orwellian doublespeak* when referring to
attacks where evil people happen to choose a gun to attack
with, these groups have created a subliminally negative
image of firearms in the mind of the general public. To
clear up the deceptive messaging by the media and
politicians and to be as transparent and forward as possible
so that we can focus on the true *root cause* of the problem,
I refer to these murderers as "rampage killers" in this book.

SERIAL KILLERS VS RAMPAGE KILLERS

Have you ever wondered why most *rampage killers* kill
themselves at the end of their rampages or that they keep
attacking until they're killed, yet *serial killers* rarely
commit suicide after they've been caught? An
overwhelming 65% of rampage shooters die in their attacks
from either being killed (17%) or committing suicide

(48%).[7] In comparison, this is not even a measurable statistic for serial killers due to its rareness. When detectives staked out the apartment building of "Son of Sam" serial killer, David Berkowitz, they waited for him to emerge from inside so that they could take him into custody. When he exited the building and was caught, Berkowitz calmly turned to one inspector and said, "I guess this is the end of the trail," giving up without so much as a cross word[8]. After a 12 month long killing spree that resulted in eight people shot and six dead, in his capture, Berkowitz was as gentle and laid-back as I am laid up on a couch with a belly full of food after a nice Thanksgiving dinner. Why the big difference between serial killers and rampage killers? The biggest reason for this difference is that these two types of killers are wired and operate differently from each other. Although it is still hotly debated, serial killers are mostly considered *psychopaths* while rampage killers are considered *sociopaths*.[9]

ANTISOCIAL PERSONALITY DISORDER

A person's personality is what makes them think, feel and behave a certain way. It is shaped by personal and life experiences as well as inherited traits — nature and nurture. But obviously not all personality traits are culturally or socially acceptable. A personality disorder is an unorthodox way of thinking, feeling and behaving that deviates from the expectations of the society, causes distress or problems, and lasts over time.[10]

| "...they would have decreased activity in the orbital cortex...these are involved in inhibition, social behavior, ethics, and morality"[11] |

In James Fallon's book "The Psychopath Inside" where he reviewed brain scans of killers, Mr. Fallon points out that "they would have decreased activity in the orbital cortex — the part of the prefrontal cortex just above the orbits, or eye sockets — and the nearby ventromedial prefrontal cortex. *These are involved in inhibition, social behavior, ethics, and morality.*"[12] While these killers had obvious physical abnormalities, they also had textbook cases of *antisocial personalty disorder.*

According to the Diagnostic And Statistical Manual Of Mental Disorders (DSM-5), antisocial personality disorder (ASPD) is defined as a "pervasive pattern of disregard for and violation of the rights of others, occurring since age 15, as indicated by three (or more) of the following:[13]

- Failure to conform to social norms with respect to lawful behaviors, as indicated by repeatedly performing acts that are grounds for arrest.

- Deceitfulness, as indicated by repeated lying, use of aliases, or conning others for personal profit or pleasure.

- Impulsivity or failure to plan ahead.

- Irritability and aggressiveness, as indicated by repeated physical fights or assaults.

- Reckless disregard for safety of self or others.

- Consistent irresponsibility, as indicated by repeated failure to sustain consistent work behavior or honor financial obligations.

- Lack of remorse, as indicated by being indifferent to or rationalizing having hurt, mistreated, or stolen from another.[14]

Nearly all of these ASPD traits can be identified in all of the rampage killers highlighted in this book.

So, is there a definitive cause of antisocial personality disorder? Not specifically. There are many commonalities that people with ASPD share that seem to shape their personalities when paired with certain environmental occurrences. Genetics plays a major role in ASPD while life changes and the impact of personal environment greatly influences the further development of it. Those environmental influencers can be childhood abuse of any kind, neglect, or trauma.[15] Adoption studies have actually shown that both adopted and biological children of parents with ASPD have an increased risk of developing ASPD themselves. These environmental influencers seem to have a much bigger impact on the formations of sociopaths as opposed to psychopaths who are thought to be *born* rather than *made*.

PSYCHOPATHS ARE BORN AND SOCIOPATHS ARE MADE

While both serial killers and rampage killers are clinically considered to have ASPD characteristics[16], they are not clinically the same and arrive at their decisions to take human life in very different ways.

Key traits that both psychopaths and sociopaths share include:[17]

- A disregard for laws and social morals.

- A disregard for the rights of others.

- A failure to feel remorse or guilt.

- A tendency to display violent or aggressive behavior.

While there are some who argue that *all* killers are psychopaths, most others agree that *psychopathy* implies a biological origin, while *sociopathy* implies an environmental link. Psychopaths are born devoid of empathy while sociopaths seem to lose the ability to care for others by experiencing traumatic life events.[18]

[...rampage killers are "made" while serial killers are already "made"...]

16

Here are some distinct differences between psychopaths and sociopaths:[19]

PSYCHOPATHS (Serial Killers)	SOCIOPATHS (Rampage Killers)
- Pretend to care	- Make it clear they do not care how others feel
- Display cold-hearted behavior	- Prone to fits of anger and rage
- Fail to recognize other people's distress	- Recognize what they are doing but rationalize their behavior
- Have relationships that are shallow and fake	- Can form emotional attachments, but it's difficult
- Maintain a normal life as a cover for criminal activity	- Cannot maintain a regular work and family life
- Fail to form genuine emotional attachments	- Behave in hot-headed and impulsive ways

The overwhelming majority of psychological research available points to the fact that sociopaths — rampage killers — are mostly a product of their environment and are "made" while psychopaths — serial killers — are mostly already "made" having been born that way regardless of future environmental influence. Further support of this theory is a 2014 review where it was noted that "as many as a third of people diagnosed with sociopathy essentially 'give up' their antisocial behavior in later life and develop well-adjusted relationships".[20] Research has even shown that moderating factors like marriage, employment, early incarceration (or adjudication during childhood), and degree of socialization has a dramatic effect on sociopaths in life.

In my opinion, this is hope that sociopaths who may be headed in the wrong direction in life can experience a correction of that course if these moderating factors change in a more positive direction so they can go on to live more peaceful, uneventful lives.

WHY DON'T WE HEAR OF MORE CASES OF YOUNG SOCIOPATHS?

You may be wondering why we don't hear much more about young people with antisocial personality disorder. According to the DSM-5, while the signs may generally be present of ASPD during childhood, one cannot be officially diagnosed with it before they turn 18. Persons under the age of 18 are typically given the distinction of "conduct disorder" instead. In order to obtain an ASPD diagnosis, a person must be 18 or older, have had conduct disorder symptoms before age 15, not have the behavior of that of bipolar disorder or schizophrenia, and must exhibit three or more of the seven traits listed above.[21]

Considering an individual can't be diagnosed with ASPD until they're 18 means that many rampage killers are never diagnosed with it because they commit their acts of atrocity before their eighteenth birthday or haven't been properly diagnosed soon enough after they turn 18. This is the case with Adam Lanza who was 20 when committing his murders and whose mother had stopped bringing him to a psychiatrist, Seung-Hui Cho who was 23 and hadn't seen a psychiatrist in years, Eric Harris who killed himself 11 days after his eighteenth birthday, and even Nikolas Cruz who somehow managed to "slip through the cracks" of the system. Although clearly sociopaths with ASPD, none of these notorious rampage killers were diagnosed as such because of the specific rules in making the diagnosis.

RAMPAGE KILLERS

My focus in this book is on sociopaths and how they're potentially "made." I look at three of the more glaring and obvious common denominators among nearly all rampage killers:

1) Being raised in broken homes.

2) Being bullied.

3) Being treated with mood-altering or psychiatric medications.

Now before people from broken homes who were bullied and on prescription medication unite to hunt me down for daring to point out these obvious commonalities, I'm going to repeat a disclaimer that you will find often in this book: *I don't imply nor make any wild assumption that any person experiencing one, two, or even all three of these events will be the next headline-grabbing rampage killer.* Just as everyone with shared traits of antisocial personality disorder doesn't grow up to be a serial killer or rampage killer, clearly not everyone who experiences these three common events I define above becomes a rampage killer. I do, however, find it particularly odd and wildly coincidental that practically all rampage killers were raised in broken homes, were bullied, and were medicated. That's irrefutable. That's a statistical fact. That's not exactly like making some broad observation that all rampage killers wear denim pants, like music, and prefer the color blue. The three traits I focus on have a direct impact on shaping the mind, the personality, and the actions of the person possessing them. It's also worth noting that it's very common to have separate variants of the exact same mental disorder appear very different to the treating physician. Clearly results may vary and they often do.

My hope is to shed some light on some of the more obvious things that often happen right before our eyes that the mainstream media misses, refuses to report on, or has a vested or ideological interest in not reporting. What's happening today is not working and no one is legitimately working towards properly determining what causal factors or events are involved in rampage killings. Blaming guns is a misdirected copout that prevents any chance of finding a solution to the problem.

CHAPTER 2: ROOT CAUSE ANALYSIS

"The rifle itself has no moral stature, since it has no will of its own. Naturally, it may be used by evil men for evil purposes, but there are more good men than evil, and while the latter cannot be persuaded to the path of righteousness by propaganda, they can certainly be corrected by good men with rifles." - *Jeff Cooper*

Before I started my own business some 18 years ago, I was fortunate enough to work in upper management at a Fortune 500 company for a number of years. Most Fortune 500 companies like to blow budget dollars on stupid meetings and pointless "workshops" just to check off individual boxes on their own annual performance reviews. The company I worked for was no different. But there was one particular workshop that wasn't worthless and I remember it well. It was one on determining *root causes* and boy was it interesting! It shaped the way I think today and taught me such simple ways to solve even the most intricate of problems. The workshop was on performing a *root cause analysis* on problems.

When presented with routinely occurring problems, any reasonable person with an average IQ will look for ways to prevent it from continuing to happen. The goal is to put a stop to future chaos. Determining root cause analysis is not some groundbreaking tactic that a super-secret, select group of people know how to miraculously complete, nor is it some high level, members-only class that only super high functioning intellectuals take with ultra-advanced degrees. No, this is common sense at its most fundamental level. Even a toddler who has stepped on a Lego in their play area will have enough sense to either walk around the Legos or pick them up in the future. The Lego lying in the middle of the floor is the root cause of why the toddler's foot hurts after stepping on it. But this basic common sense approach to problem-solving gets in the way of many politicians and opportunistic individuals with nefarious political agendas time and time again.

| *If the root cause of a problem is never sought out...you aren't serious about solving the problem.* |

If your teenager is continuously wrecking all of the family cars, taking the teen's own car away from them may serve as punishment for their actions, but it certainly doesn't identify nor prevent them from wrecking a car again. It *pauses* the problem rather than solving or preventing it. The problem is still there. The responsible thing to do is to perform an analysis of their situation in order to determine the root cause of their problem. We want to see whether or not they're texting while driving, if they have poor eyesight, or if they're impaired in any way while driving. It would be lazy and pointless to just take the car away. It's obvious that the true root cause exists with the individual driving the car into things they're not supposed to and not with the car that is sitting idly in the driveway. By identifying the root cause as poor eyesight, the parents can now get corrective lenses for the teen to make them a safer driver and in turn, stop wrecking vehicles.

If the root cause of a problem is never properly sought out, it can never be solved. No one in any position should ever complain or comment about a problem if they aren't looking for the actual root cause, because clearly they aren't serious about solving the problem in the first place.

But in spite of average, everyday people like you and I recognizing the proper way to identify and solve problems, the anti-gun enterprise and the well paid anti-gun politicians see rampage killings happening over and over again with the same root causes and are either too lazy or too stupid to identify them — take your pick of either one. Rather than trying to identify the reasons why people make the decision to kill other humans, they propose instead to disenfranchise millions upon millions of innocent, law-abiding Americans by attempting to limit their constitutional rights. That's as stupid as banning boats in order to stop shark attacks.

MANAGE IT OR IT MANAGES YOU

To understand the process of determining a true root cause, it's important to understand two very different types of management styles and approaches — *reactive* and *proactive* management.

Reactive management tends to wait for problems to reveal themselves and then work towards resolving them by eliminating or treating symptoms that are a result of their manifestation. The same problems can occur again in the future and the same treatment of their symptoms would again take place to resolve them. They wait for the problem to produce itself and then they react to it. This style is much more defensive and has the manager essentially putting out fires as they pop up while never eliminating any reoccurring problems.

| *Proactive management…is more of an offensive approach that essentially hunts the problem down and extinguishes it.* |

By contrast, proactive management is geared towards preventing the problems before they ever occur. It does this by identifying the root cause — the *main* cause — of problems that have occurred in the past and then working to develop corrective actions that prevent them from reoccurring. This is more of an offensive approach that essentially hunts the problem down and extinguishes it before it can happen again.

One of the most important tools in the proactive approach is *event correlation*. Event correlation is the analysis of a number of events that are common during problems as they occur, the elimination of irrelevant events, a statistical summary of remaining events, and the determination of whether or not some events impact others or can be explained by others.

THE 5 WHYS

When determining the root cause analysis of a problem, we look for events or causal factors that contribute to the creation of the overall problem. To simplify it: causal factors are the events that contribute to the root cause.

To narrow down these important causal factors, a very helpful exercise in performing a root cause analysis is to determine the *5 whys*. This may involve — in the case of the teenager and the wrecked cars — asking:

FIRST WHY: "Why is your car dented?"
ANSWER: "I ran into a utility pole."

SECOND WHY: "Why did you run into a utility pole?"
ANSWER: "Because I never saw it."

THIRD WHY: "Why didn't you see it?"
ANSWER: "Because my vision is blurry."

FOURTH WHY: "Why is your vision blurry?"
ANSWER: "Maybe because I need corrective lenses or glasses."

BOOM! After only 4 whys we've got our root cause - poor eyesight. It may not have been 5 whys, but that number is arbitrary. Past experience has shown that 5 whys will typically lead to the root cause. But it can be more than 5 or less than 5. While this exercise may feel like the overly inquisitive toddler asking a string of endless whys, it's very effective at drilling down to the real cause in one of the simplest of ways.

So, can we say with any level of confidence that the existence of firearms of any kind is the root cause of rampage killings? Let's see…

FIRST WHY: "Why is that person dead?"
ANSWER: "He was shot with a firearm."

SECOND WHY: "Why was he shot with a firearm?"
ANSWER: "The killer was upset/angry."

After only 2 whys we are already beyond the issue of the instrument used to kill the person and continuing on to determine the true root cause of the death. We'll ask more whys regarding rampage killers in Chapter 7.

ARE POLITICIANS AND THE MEDIA STUPID OR COMMITTED IDEOLOGUES?

Every *successful* business in history has benefitted from properly conducting root cause analyses at some point, whether they knew they were doing it or not. Oddly, the United States government cannot seem to grasp this simple problem-solving concept even after being "in business" for over 245 years. It almost gives the appearance that they're too incompetent to solve social problems or else they don't really *want* to solve the problems that they're paid handsomely to attack in the media.

Every time there is a high profile rampage killing, the well paid, anti-gun politicians flock like cockroaches to any cameraman that will shine a light on them so that they can pretend to care as they repeat every unrelated, misguided, anti-constitutional talking point that their check-writing lobbyists have manufactured and prepared for them. But not once has one of them asked "what is the root cause of these killings so that we can prevent the next one?" Not once have they asked that. Instead, they wait with great anticipation — and sometimes just make it up — to see what kind of gun was used in the murders so that they can plead in their super-duper, really sad voice "why does anyone need a [*fill in the blank*] gun anyway?" These politicians are the epitome of the parent taking the car away from the teenager to stop them from wrecking other cars. Even the toddler who stepped on the Lego isn't stupid enough to think making guns inaccessible to honest, law-abiding Americans will prevent a wacko from deciding to kill other people. It's absurd to state otherwise.

Let's look at all the annual deaths in America that are far greater in number than those committed by people with firearms and apply the same twisted, anti-gun logic:

When 655,381 Americans die each year from heart disease[22], we don't try to make it harder for fried chicken joints to sell fried chicken to law-abiding Americans.

When 599,274 Americans die each year from cancer[23], billionaires don't create lobbyist groups called Every Mom For Sun Screen Action to march on Washington D.C.

When 440,000 Americans die each year of medical malpractice[24], no one calls for stricter background checks for doctors.

When 159,486 Americans die each year from chronic lower respiratory diseases[25], politicians don't call for a waiting period for people to smoke cigarettes they want to purchase.

When 122,019 Americans die each year from diabetes[26], no one tries to limit the size of donut boxes or limit how many donuts one can buy at one time.

But when 11,078 Americans are murdered each year with a firearm[27], not one politician or lobbyist group asks what makes people want to kill other people so we can stop it.

In the following chapters you'll see all the data I used to determine the root cause analysis of rampage killers. More specifically, you'll see my event correlation of the circumstances that have taken place along the story line of several of these killers in recent history.

CHAPTER 3: BROKEN HOMES

A study of adolescents convicted of homicide in adult court found that at the time of their crimes, less than 20% of them were from married parent households.[28]

A solid family unit has always been the fundamental building block of any society. Through the naturally occurring bonding with their parents, children internalize the moral values that are likely to shape their future conduct. But as we all know, preserving the traditional nuclear family unit can many times be a lost cause and that battle has gotten harder and harder to win these days. The chance that a child will reach adulthood after being raised by his or her biological parents has never been lower than it is today.[29] The age of the *broken home* is upon us.

WHAT IS A BROKEN HOME?

The term "broken home" entered the English language in the mid-1800s to describe the absence of one parent for any unfortunate reason, including prolonged illness, incarceration, or extreme poverty. Use of the term rose during the first half of the 20th century, peaking in the 1950s, but began to decline by the 1970s.[30]

For the purpose of this book, I'm going to include many other things that fall under the term "broken home" because

I believe that there are far more stressors and impactful things that contribute to a broken home than simply one of two parents missing. My updated definition includes:

- **Single parent homes** - One of either the mother or father is not present in the home.

- **Alcohol, illegal drugs, or prescription drug abuse** - Children of substance abusing parents are at risk of a wide variety of other negative outcomes, including emotional, social, and behavioral adjustment problems as well as challenges in cognitive and academic functioning.[31]

- **Physical, emotional, or sexual abuse** - Children who witness or are victims of emotional, physical, or sexual abuse are at higher risk for mental health problems as adults.[32]

- **Infidelity** - 70% of adult children that came from families where one parent was unfaithful said they believe it impacted their ability to trust others.[33]

- **Criminal behavior** - In a longitudinal study of 394 families in England, fewer than 5% of the families accounted for almost half of the criminal convictions in the entire sample. Delinquency can most certainly be transmitted from one generation to the next.[34]

- **"Absent" parents** - Sometimes being present in the home is the same as not being there at all. Some parents "live" at home, but don't participate in raising their children.

| 75% of the most notorious school shooters in recent history were raised in broken homes.[35] |

Essentially, I see a broken home as a home where no negative influences exist that can psychologically impact the development of a member of the family. Many times these stressors have a huge impact. There is solid evidence that youth from single, divorced, criminal or imprisoned parents, are less likely to follow standard life courses.[36] When I use these criteria for defining a broken home, statistics show that 75% of the most notorious school shooters in recent history were raised in broken homes.[37]

Neuroscientists have actually shown that early adversity — such as a very chaotic and frightening home life — can result in a young child becoming hyper vigilant to potential threats in their environment. This appears to influence the development of brain connectivity and functions. Such children may enter adolescence with brain systems that are set differently and this may increase their likelihood of taking impulsive risks. For many young offenders, such early adversity is a common experience and it may increase both their vulnerability to mental health problems and also their risk of problem behaviors.[38]

A 1987 study proposed that inept family socialization leads to trivial antisocial behaviors in children. These antisocial behaviors and lack of social skills lead to rejection by teachers and students, pushing the child into gravitating towards other antisocial or socially inept youths. The study viewed delinquency as an "end-product of inadequate socialization whose roots can be observed in childhood".[39] What happens to children who are rejected in social settings? They are many times ostracized or bullied.

None of the stressors I've identified as part of a broken home should be minimized or downplayed as one being better or worse than the other. But there's no denying that some certainly have a much bigger impact on the development of our youth than others. One of the most impactful is growing up in a single parent home — more specifically, a fatherless home. Studies show that growing up in a fatherless home has by far the biggest negative impact on a child's development. It's also overwhelmingly common amongst rampage killers.

ARE LOW INCOME HOUSEHOLDS PART OF THE PROBLEM?

While low income homes can be negative influencers in a home setting, it doesn't have the same psychological effect on a young person's psyche as it would in a home where they may otherwise be physically abused or where they observe morally devoid behavior. I personally grew up in a low income household — albeit one that was intact and happy — and I experienced no negative psychological effects of being poor, nor did the lack of finances cause any illicit behavior within our home.

As with most anything else, politicians dabble in fields they have no business dabbling in and this is another one of them. Many lawmakers at the federal and state level make the incorrect assumption that crime is negatively affected by low income households. But since 1965, welfare spending in low income areas has increased by over 800%, while the number of major felonies per capita in 1995 was roughly three times the rate before 1960.[40] Clearly throwing money at this problem hasn't helped reduce crime even in the slightest measurable way. But the politicians will just tell you that they need even more money to throw at the problem if they are going to have any real chance at making a difference.

MY TWO-PARENT HOME

As mentioned above, I grew up in a low income home with both parents present. My dad was a very low-key, quiet man. He never raised his voice or made a big deal out of anything. He was the owner of a small, independent mechanic shop. He was the worst kind of small business owner — the kind type. People took advantage of my dad's kindness. But he was liked and respected and I think that made him happy. My mom, on the other hand, ruled our household with an iron fist. I think people feared getting on her bad side more than they may have respected her. But she was a good person. My brother, my two sisters, and myself were loved. We honestly didn't realize we were poor until we'd go to someone else's house who wasn't. We didn't *feel* poor. We may not have had all the cool toys that the more well-off kids had, but we never went hungry. Ever.

One of the most memorable things I can remember growing up is learning how to act and how to treat other people through watching my parents interact with others. My dad never sat us down to lecture us on how to do these things or treat people. We learned by watching him. I watched as he'd greet other men with a firm handshake and a smile. I watched as he'd open doors for ladies and call them "ma'am". I watched as he'd acknowledge little kids and make them feel special. I learned by watching him. He died suddenly when I was 23 years old and I miss him dearly. But he was there in those very formative years and I know what I took from that.

Our family wasn't perfect. But our parents loved us and did the best they could for us. Research confirms that children raised in supportive, affectionate, and accepting homes are less likely to become deviant. Children rejected by parents are among the most likely to become delinquent. According to professional studies, the absence of the father is the single most important cause of poverty. The same is true for crime.[41]

FATHERLESS HOMES

Clearly both parents in a home are equally important. Nobody is suggesting one is better than the other. And I'm not just saying that to cover my tail with those nutty "woman are better at everything" kooks. I wouldn't be the person I am today without my dad *and* my mom. But rampage killers are mostly boys or men and — regardless of what some wacko, feel-good, pseudo-intellectual might tell us — there are some things that a growing boy can *only* learn from a man in the house.

The benefits a child receives from his relationship with his father are notably different from those derived from his relationship with his mother. The father contributes a sense of paternal authority and discipline which is conveyed through his involved presence. The additional benefits of his affection and attachment add to this primary benefit.[42]

Here are some facts I've gathered through my research on the effects a fatherless home has on young men:

- Boys who are fatherless from birth are a whopping three times as likely to go to jail as peers from intact families, while boys whose fathers do not leave until they are 10 to 14 years old are two times as likely to go to jail as their peers from intact families.[43]

- The rate of violent teenage crime corresponds with the number of families abandoned by fathers.[44]

- A boy abandoned by his father is deprived of a deep sense of personal security.[45]

- 85% of youth who are currently in prison grew up in a fatherless home.[46]

- Living in a fatherless home is a contributing factor to substance abuse, with children from such homes accounting for 75% of adolescent patients being treated in substance abuse centers.[47]

- 63% of youth suicides involve a child who was living in a fatherless home when they made their final decision.[48]

- Children who live in a fatherless home are 279% more likely to deal drugs or carry firearms for offensive purposes compared to children who live with their fathers.[49]

| *85% of youth who are currently in prison grew up in a fatherless home.* |

And by contrast, studies have shown that a close and intense relationship between a boy and his father prevents hostility and inappropriate aggressiveness.[50] The very presence of the father embodies authority, an authority conveyed through his daily involvement in family life. This paternal authority is critical to the prevention of psychopathology and delinquency.[51]

Simply put: a boy needs his father in his life. I don't care whose feelings this hurts. For most of the single moms out there, I know you're doing your best and I love you for that. But we cannot deny or ignore this glaring fact simply because we are worried about hurting someone's feelings who this may apply to.

SO, WHY IS NONE OF THIS NEWS?

If all of these disturbing statistics exist whenever children are raised in fatherless homes, why don't we hear more about it? Why aren't there committees/sub-committees/task forces being put together to encourage preserving the family unit? Why isn't this front-page news?

These days, the mainstream media is so afraid of offending anyone in the latest, trendy, imbecilic, protected class that they would sacrifice their own first born to still be viewed as "inclusive" and "progressive." Remember, we're currently right in the middle of the "women-are-better-than-men-at-everything" campaign, so if one were to point out that a biological man was the main component missing in the traditional family setting, the wacko PC Police and their entire world would implode.

Take, for example, mainstream media's 2018 attack of former Republican senator from Pennsylvania, Rick Santorum, when they piled on him saying, "current Senior CNN Political Commentator Rick Santorum's response to gun violence is to attack single mothers" when all

Santorum had stated on CNN was, "We want to talk about things we can work together on? How about working together to try to see what we can do to get more dads involved in the lives of the kids." While Santorum's comment was simply pro-family and clearly not anti-woman, the media chose to virtue signal for ratings rather than performing actual "journalism" where they would have found scientific data to support Santorum's claim.

| *"We want to talk about things we can work together on? How about working together to try to see what we can do to get more dads involved in the lives of the kids."*
- Rick Santorum |

Santorum was no more claiming that single mothers are creating "gun violence" anymore than I'm suggesting that broken homes create rampage killers. But to ignore the empirical evidence that proves fatherless homes do have a direct, negative impact on the lives of rampage killers is choosing to be ignorant on this topic. Today's "media" have abandoned any semblance of journalism in their eager desire to fit in and be accepted by their group-thinking peers and we should stop expecting anything different from them. Facts get in the way of their agendas.

It's very possible that the screwballs pushing the "coolness" of single parenting may be doing more harm than good by encouraging so many of the weak-minded group-thinkers in American society to not even attempt to preserve their own family unit with the payout to them being seen as "cool" while ignoring any effects their virtue signaling may be having on their own children. But there's more payout to them — *actual payout.*

One big incentive created by the federal government to reward people for not getting married and rewards them for staying single is the *marriage tax penalty.* In a nutshell, a couple incurs a marriage penalty if the two pay more income tax filing as a married couple than they would pay if they were single and filed as individuals.[52]

The next incentive — and the biggest — is the U.S. welfare system. The welfare system is essentially a contract between the government and single mothers to create babies for money. And this is a very lucrative business to be in. The only requirements are to 1) have babies, 2) don't get married, and 3) don't get a job. The contorted welfare system of America is at the root of so many societal issues that plague the country today and politicians are happy to keep the system unchanged. By maintaining the system as-is, the government cultivates a heavy sense of dependency on the federal government by the individual while making them think they're working to give the people something good in return. This ensures votes for those politicians. This system also keeps lower income districts completely discombobulated and in disarray so that the politicians can swoop in and offer more free stuff to "help". This is the same sick concept of a person who beats their dog and then dresses the dog's wounds.

BROKEN HOMES AS A CAUSAL FACTOR

Here's one more eye-popping fact on broken homes: every single rampage killer I investigated was raised in a home that contained either a single parent, alcohol or drug abuse, physical/emotional/sexual abuse, infidelity, criminal behavior, or an absent parent. At what point do we stop calling it a coincidence and start calling it a trend?

Many parents today do their very best to combat these various challenges of why homes are broken. Parenting isn't easy. But sadly, not accepting ones parenting responsibilities *is* easy. No family is perfect. But as leaders of our own households we must be able to view our own families with a critical eye and recognize when there's an issue and then work to resolve it by any means possible. Our children's futures depends on the decisions we make in the face of this adversity.

Growing up in a broken home opens the door to the two other main causal factors I discuss in detail in this book — bullied kids and over-medicated kids. A broken home is where so many things that need fixing were first broken.

Broken homes are clear cut causal factors regarding rampage killers.

CHAPTER 4: BULLYING

"If people would give me more compliments all of this might still be avoidable... but probably not. Whatever I do people make fun of me, and sometimes directly to my face. I'll get revenge soon enough. Fuckers shouldn't have ripped on me so much huh!" — *Eric Harris / Columbine School Shooter*

When I was born my feet faced inward towards each other in an extreme pigeon-toed-like manner. Shortly after I was born, doctors bent my feet outward and put a pair of little shoes on my feet with a bar affixed between them. The setup was meant to bend my feet and legs into their correct position and then continue to grow that way. This was 1968. I doubt they do it this way anymore.

For the first 10 years of my life I wore "corrective" shoes. These were big clunky, leather shoes with somewhat thick soles that were intended to somehow help my feet grow properly. As a youngster I stood out amongst sneakers and athletic shoe-wearing kids. But it didn't seem to matter that I was different and I still felt included and equal to all other kids on the playground and in the classroom.

Then came third grade at F.K. White Middle School in Lake Charles, LA. I remember being in the boy's bathroom one day and this fifth grade kid started making fun of my shoes. "Nice shoes," and some other cracks about them. I didn't understand why this was happening. I couldn't

41

process why this older kid was concerned with my shoes and felt the need to try to make me feel bad about them. It didn't make sense to me. Was he mad at me? Had I done him wrong in some way? Why did he care that I had to wear these stupid, corrective shoes? Didn't he know that I hadn't *chosen* to wear these big, ugly, clunky shoes?

That was my first time experiencing bullying and the first time having it directed at me. I distinctly remember how it made me feel — *bad*. My feelings were hurt. I felt stupid and confused. I wondered if everyone who saw my stupid shoes felt like that about them. Was it just that no one was telling me? It was the first time in my life that I really remember feeling sad. I can remember the older kid had really curly hair and wore bell bottom type pants. Now I'm 53 years old as I write this and I can still remember those details from 45 years ago. I remember those details because that moment is forever burned into my memory. Being the target of bullying introduces one to a whole new set of emotions that aren't felt in any other circumstance. It's a weird combination of sadness, anger, shame, loneliness, and emptiness that if you've never experienced it, you don't want to.

THE BULLING EPIDEMIC IN AMERICA TODAY

My bullying experiences were minor in comparison to what I witnessed happening to other kids over the years. I was lucky that I was a tall kid and with most bullies being cowards, they backed off when I didn't take what they were dishing out. Other kids were not so lucky. I saw kids get sucked into fights they didn't want to be in. I saw teachers look the other way when kids were picked on. I even saw teachers bully kids. I was once threatened by an older kid when I spoke up for a younger kid getting bullied. I saw kids who looked broken as a result of the constant bullying they endured.

If you are reading this, you've surely either been bullied, you've bullied someone else, or you know someone who's been bullied. And you would not be alone. Here are some incredibly sad statistics regarding this disgusting epidemic:

- 49% of children in grades 4 through 12 reported being bullied by other students at school at least once during the past month.[53]

- 282,000 students are physically assaulted each month in some way in secondary schools.[54]

- 64% of students who are bullied do not report it.[55]

- 71% of young people say they've witnessed bullying at school.[56]

- 70% of school staff report they've seen bullying.[57]

- Approximately 30% of young people admit to bullying others at one time or another.[58]

- Over 160,000 kids refuse to go to school each day for fear of being bullied.[59]

- Over 10% of students who drop out of school do so due to being bullied repeatedly.[60]

- 90% of students in grades 4-8 report having been harassed or bullied.[61]

| 90% of students in grades 4-8 report having been harassed or bullied.[62] |

With stats like this, how do we as Americans simply ignore what's happening right before our eyes? This is completely unacceptable. Maybe we should do something, like maybe pass legislation to help prevent bullying. Oh, wait, we have and it's actually made things worse! I give you the infamous, ill-conceived "zero tolerance" policy.

ZERO TOLERANCE POLICIES PROTECT BULLIES

For those who overcome bullying like myself, it really does make you stronger. By the time I got into middle school I actually looked for that fifth grader who'd bullied me in third grade. Why? Because I was going to kick his ass! Instead of wallowing in despair, this kid's bullying had hardened me and taught me that I would never let that lingering group of emotions torture me again. I realized that I'd had rather confront the bully and get my butt kicked back then than to have to live with and deal with the roller coaster of emotions by just letting it go. Sorry, but I don't think "just letting it go" solves anything when it comes to bullying. I think it makes it worse for both parties. The bullied carries regret and sadness while the bully gets even more emboldened and moves on to bully another kid. But how can a young person being bullied deter the bully with today's ridiculous "zero tolerance" policies in effect?

| Sorry, but I don't think "just letting it go" solves anything when it comes to bullying. |

Zero tolerance refers to school discipline policies and practices that mandate predetermined consequences — typically severe — in response to specific types of student misbehavior, regardless of the context or rationale for the behavior. The term originated in the Reagan era during which the federal Anti-Drug Abuse Act of 1986 was signed into law as a response to the War on Drugs. The law imposed new mandatory minimum sentences for drug offenders changing a rehabilitative system into a punitive system. Then Congress passed the Gun-Free Schools Act of 1994, requiring states to expel students who bring firearms to school. It was originally intended as a response to serious offenses like selling drugs or engaging in gang-related fights on school grounds and was meant to ensure safe and healthy schools. However, in recent years zero tolerance policies have been applied broadly to include minor offenses like talking back to school personnel, bringing over-the-counter or prescription drugs on school grounds without a doctor's note, and coming to school out of uniform. Research has shown that zero tolerance policies can cause harmful effects to individuals, lead to higher rates of exclusionary disciplinary action, and are not associated with improved school safety and academics.[63]

One of the biggest problems with the ridiculous and lazy disciplinary arm of zero tolerance is that a bully can pick on another child endlessly and as long as the conflict doesn't escalate. At that point, everything is fine — for the bully. The bully gets to keep bullying and the bullied keeps getting bullied. But if the bullied child decides to strike

45

back and end the torment, he — along with the bully — will be expelled. The circumstances that led up to the child defending himself have no bearing on the punishment. *Zero tolerance* means *zero logic and reasoning* will be employed in these instances. It's easy for lazy school administrators to implement zero tolerance. It requires no additional work and no thinking. And there's no threat of a parent getting angry because — "hey, I'm just doing my job, man!"

Now let's think about this for a moment: some dead end kid gets to pick on an innocent kid and if the innocent kid dares to defend himself he'll get kicked out of school. It sounds stupid to even say that out loud. But think for a minute what we're doing to that bullied kid. We're forcing him to allow himself to be devalued on a daily basis while internalizing the hurt and rage produced from the constant bullying. I mean, if he even goes to a teacher or school official to report the bullying — which as we stated earlier, most don't — the teacher or school official will just casually mention something to the bully, only making it tougher on the bullied kid the next time they run in to each other. There's no way the bullied kid can win in this situation. And the bully wins no matter what! By not getting rightfully punched in the throat by the kid he's bullying, he gets to assume this "king of the hill" type status in the eyes of all the other kids. And if the bullying kid does throat punch him, they both get expelled and he looks cool for it. You think he cares about being expelled? Hell no he doesn't care! He's already a loser and was only bullying for attention anyway. But the kid getting bullied may have been a good student with good grades and a bright future and now he's lost all of that.

IT'S NOT JUST THE KIDS

Eric Harris from Columbine notoriety wrote in his suicide note:

"Parents and teachers, you fucked up. You have taught these kids to not accept what is different. YOU ARE IN THE WRONG. I have taken their lives and my own—but it was your doing. Teachers, parents, LET THIS MASSACRE BE ON YOUR SHOULDERS UNTIL THE DAY YOU DIE."[64]

Here are some statistics on teacher-involved bullying:

- 2% of middle school students report being bullied by a teacher.

- 30% of secondary students report being bullied by a teacher.

- 64% of young adults report being bullied by a teacher at least once over the course of their lifetime.

- 93% of high school and college students identified at least one teacher as a bully in their school.

These statistics are unacceptable for adults! It angers me to know that adults contribute negatively to these kids' mental health problems and are never held accountable for it. I'll use the phrase "you're old enough to know better." I watched teachers and even a coach one time directly witness bullying and literally turn away from it and do nothing about it. Many times these bullied kids see that these figures of authority allow the bullying to happen which makes the young person feel even more isolated and alone. Imagine the betrayal a young person feels in an instance like that. I know many awesome teachers and coaches, but I also know and have dealt with teachers and coaches who I wouldn't leave a parakeet in the protective custody of. Some of these teachers and coaches were probably bullied themselves in school and now because they're in a position of authority, they're part of the "in crowd." Shedding the baggage they carried for years of not being "cool." This is sad and pathetic.

BULLYING'S EFFECTS ON SUICIDE (...AND HOMICIDE)

Just as so many things have to align perfectly for the making of a monster, the relationship and link between bullying and suicide or homicide is complex and not simple enough to condense into a few pages in this book. I also don't want to imply that all kids that are bullied immediately become rampage killers. I didn't become one. I'd say that the overwhelming majority of children who are bullied will be just fine. But to deny that bullying can push that one person past the point of breaking and taking his or her own life or a number of others' lives would be irresponsible and factually incorrect based on all the data available to prove otherwise.

| *87% of students surveyed report that they feel bullying is the primary motivator of school shootings.* |

Research indicates that persistent bullying of a young person can worsen feelings of isolation, rejection, exclusion, and despair, as well as depression and anxiety,

48

which may lead to suicidal behavior.[65] Statistics also suggest that revenge due to bullying is the number one motivator for school shootings in the United States. Nearly 75% of school shootings have been linked to harassment and bullying. 87% of students surveyed report that they feel bullying is the primary motivator of school shootings.[66]

Another thing that helps explain bullied children becoming rampage killers is the fact that bullying is a group phenomenon. Rarely do we see bullies picking on a person all by themselves unless it's a continuation of previous bullying where the two parties just happen to be alone. Bullying is rarely just peer to peer because the bully is bullying to acquire attention and standing among those witnessing the act. It's essentially a show to establish a form of dominance within a particular group. This could explain why rampage shooters typically don't just target one person and instead focus on larger groups. In their minds — while the bystanders (and teachers/faculty) may not have bullied them — those people did nothing to stop the bullying, so they're viewed as complicit.

To be clear, *the vast majority of young people who are bullied do not become suicidal or homicidal.* As I explain in this book, there are multiple risk factors that have an effect on a child resorting to suicide or homicide.

In so many cases bullying leads to anxiety and depression, resulting in medical treatment for these bullied children. These are all the steps necessary for building the perfect monster. The next chapter takes us into the world of overmedicated children.

SO, WHY IS THIS IN A BOOK ON RAMPAGE KILLERS?

According to assistant professor of sociology and criminology at Adelphi University, Jessie Klein, "Almost every school shooter in cases studied over the last decade cited bullying as a motivating factor for the crime."[67] Now of course we hear attempts at debunking this claim, but those opposing claims are almost always traced back to the school and school district being sued by victims' families for allowing and even promoting the bullying efforts that triggered a school shooter. For example, there were inaccurate claims that Eric Harris (Columbine) and Nikolas Cruz (Parkland) weren't bullied, but these were prompted by lawsuits and deemed inaccurate by actual eye witnesses.

My point here is that in many cases, administrators and faculty — and even students — could help many of these socially awkward kids simply by recognizing signs and being vocal about them to their peers. Acceptance by peers and simply not being bullied could prevent a kid from diving deeper into a world of depression and despair. It could also help keep some of these kids off of mood altering drugs that are negatively rewiring their developing, young brains.

CHAPTER 5: NO CHILD LEFT BEHIND'S COLLATERAL DAMAGE

"I used to love teaching. Four words drove me into retirement—No Child Left Behind. I could no longer attend to the needs and wants of my students. All I was supposed to do was to get them ready to take tests." — *Steve Eklund (Retired teacher)*[68]

The "No Child Left Behind" Act of 2001 was a bipartisan act passed by the U.S. Congress in 2001 and it reauthorized the "Elementary and Secondary Education Act" by promoting standards-based education reform and setting new curriculums that was meant to improve standards and individual performances. Since education is not included in the U.S. Constitution, which *should* prevent the federal government from trying to control education directives, this was the federal government's way to essentially bribe individual states with U.S. taxpayer money by pressing them to develop basic skill programs and present them to the U.S. government for approval in order to receive said tax dollars.

No Child Left Behind was largely a failed pay-for-performance system that restricted teachers' individual ability to be creative in their teaching efforts, while dehumanizing students by creating a test-obsessed system. Teachers were pressed to teach students to pass specific tests so that their schools would get an acceptable evaluation in the government's eyes. The prize wasn't the satisfaction of helping children learn in whichever manner they needed to learn anymore. The prize was now simply money. Meanwhile, a well-rounded and complete curriculum was abandoned for a small subset of specific topics that focused on just what was going to be administered on the standardized tests.

| *The prize wasn't the satisfaction of helping children learn in whichever manner they needed to learn anymore. The prize was now simply money.* |

So, the schools whose students performed well on the standardized tests got a pile of money. But what did the "losers" of the NCLB lottery get?

THE MEANS TO AN END

If a school's results under No Child Left Behind was repeatedly bad, then steps were mandated to improve the school and staff itself. Those steps — depending on how many years in a row test scores were unacceptable — could include developing plans to improve on teaching specific subjects, students being eligible to transfer to better performing schools, tutoring services being offered to students, entire staffs being replaced, and even schools being closed down completely. These last two items are very problematic. By penalizing teachers and administrators with their jobs, an incentive to corrupt the system was born. Teachers and administrators now went from being morally driven to do the right thing for the sake of educating children to now being financially driven to figure out how to improve the test scores the children — and the schools — were being evaluated on.

While I don't condone corruption and deceit, I do understand what drives some people to employ corrupt measures when their very livelihood is threatened. While the No Child Left Behind model was clearly flawed — better performing schools received more money to continue improving and poorer performing schools received no help — it made adults feel the need to figure out how to game the system or risk not putting food on their own family's table. I'm a huge proponent of accountability in one's job and their own actions. But when you make a goal unachievable based on what one can actually control, you have incentivized those affected with finding ways to gain the control they need to affect the outcome.

IDENTIFYING THE CHILDREN CAUSING THE LOWER TEST SCORES

According to the Center For Disease Control (CDC), "Attention-deficit/hyperactivity disorder (ADHD) is one of the most common neurodevelopmental disorders of childhood, affecting more than 6.4 million US children aged 4–17 years. Although ADHD is usually first diagnosed in childhood, it often lasts into adulthood. ADHD is a serious public health concern because of its high prevalence; chronic nature; significant impact on school performance, family life, and peer relationships; and estimated annual cross-sector costs of $38–72 billion. ADHD cannot be cured, but many treatment options exist, including parent training, school accommodations and interventions, medications, and behavioral intervention strategies."

Teachers and administrators were quick to identify which children were keeping cumulative standardized test scores down. Many of those children — because they *are* children — exhibited signs of ADHD like difficulty paying attention. Fearing for their own jobs as a result of poor or potentially declining test scores, is it *possible* that teachers and administrators began recommending that these children receive treatment for their symptoms to settle them down and to help them focus — and to score better on standardized tests?

Another incentive for teachers and administrators to push as many children as possible into the ADHD bubble was the fact that in 1991, children diagnosed with ADHD could be included under the Individuals with Disabilities Education Act which allowed these children more time than their peers to take standardized tests and allowed them to receive free tutoring — all of which should lead to better test scores.[69]

| *...children diagnosed with ADHD could be included under the Individuals with Disabilities Education*

Act which allowed these children more time than their peers to take standardized tests and allowed them to receive free tutoring... |

No Child Left Behind was implemented in 2002. According to the CDC, by 2011 11% of all U.S. children ages 4-17 (6.4 million kids) were diagnosed with ADHD with rates up 66% from 2002 in 2012.[70] While there are non-medicinal behavior therapy treatments available to treat ADHD, most children are automatically treated with stimulants, which contain various forms of methylphenidate and amphetamine meant to calm hyperactive children. Of those 6.4 million American children diagnosed with ADHD, 70% of them ended up receiving these medications.[71] Remember that all of these medications have "black box warnings" on them that include warnings of "psychotic episodes" and "depression." Documented warnings of the most popular ADHD drug used — Dexmethylphenidatenot (Focalin) — include:

- Particular care should be taken in using stimulants to treat ADHD patients with comorbid bipolar disorder because of concern for possible induction of mixed/manic episode in such patients;[72]

- Aggressive behavior or hostility is often observed in children and adolescents with ADHD, and has been reported;[73]

- Use caution in patients with preexisting psychosis; stimulants may exacerbate symptoms of behavior and though disorder; use with caution in patients with bipolar disorder; stimulants may induce mixed/manic episodes; new onset of psychosis or mania may occur in children or adolescents with stimulant use; patients presenting with depressive symptoms should be screened for bipolar disorder, including family history of suicide, bipolar disorder, and depression; consider discontinuation of therapy if symptoms of psychosis develop;[74]

- Abrupt discontinuation following high doses or prolonged periods may result in symptoms of withdrawal including severe depression;[75]

That's 4.4 million American children on these medications.

MEDICATED KIDS BEGET DEPRESSION AND SUICIDE

Research has shown that 18% of children diagnosed early with ADHD suffered from depression. That's 10 times higher than children without ADHD. Shockingly, children with ADHD were twice as likely to have attempted suicide than those without it.[76]

Curiously, what was missing from this research was the potential correlation of the mood altering drugs with "black box warning labels"[77] that nearly all children with ADHD are prescribed that have been proven to increase depression and suicidal thoughts in those taking them. The obvious question is, is it really the ADHD that causes the depression in these kids or is *quite possibly* the psychotropic drugs used to treat the ADHD that is causing the depression — as the black box warning labels on them suggest? In an attempt to minimize the prevalence of suicidal tendencies, one of these researchers even went so far as to state that "suicide attempts were relatively rare, even in the study group."[78]

Clearly all children and even adults on ADHD medications don't have suicidal thoughts. But to ignore the fact that some do and then attempt to blame their ADHD on their psychotic thoughts is not only wrong, but puts a much worse stigma on these children and adults than they may already be labeled with.

AFTER MEDICATING 4.4 MILLION AMERICAN CHILDREN...

So, was No Child Left Behind worth it? No. Not even close. At best, fourth grade and eighth grade students had a slight bump in their math scores while hardly any impact was felt on reading scores. In 2008, after six years of NCLB, it was reported that 40% of college freshman students still required remedial courses.[79] We as Americans went along with the medicating of 4.4 million school-aged children and in return we got, for the most part, a mild uptick in math skills.

57

| ...after six years of NCLB, it was reported that 40% of college freshman students still required remedial courses.[80] |

Did we learn anything from the failures of No Child Left Behind? Did we learn anything by trying to "reinvent the wheel" in terms of education? Did we learn anything about how children are individuals and that "one size fits all" education curriculums are complete garbage? Nope.

In 2010, the Bill and Melinda Gates Foundation bankrolled the cumbersome, confusing, and highly controversial Common Core State Standards program to the tune of $200 million. In order to gain bipartisan national support along with that of the American Federation of Teachers, the National Education Association, and even organizations such as the U.S. Chamber of Commerce,[81] the Gates Foundation unloaded a small fortune to make all participants happy — at least financially speaking. Once again, our children's futures across the United States of America are sacrificed for immediate financial gain for those in power, proving again that government assistance is never about *assistance*.

And doubling down on their failure, the Every Student Succeeds Act was passed by Congress in 2015 to "replace" the failed No Child Left Behind Act. Unfortunately, the name of the act was the only wholesale change that took place here. A curriculum based on standardized testing remained in place. My fear in not making adequate changes in this flawed model when we have the opportunity is that there are many really good teachers out there who will not be corrupted by this incentive-driven system and will choose to opt out of the profession altogether at some point. These are the educators that we absolutely cannot afford to lose because they are doing what they do because they love the children and the satisfaction of teaching the children, rather than "teaching to the test."

It's important that I point out that I personally have the utmost respect for many "educators", but not all of them. Just like not all law enforcement are good *or* bad, the same is true for educators and all other professions. Some of my favorite people and friends are teachers and administrators in the school system or were at some point. Good teachers have had a huge impact on me as a young person growing up. But to give sainthood to a person simply for choosing teaching as a professional is just stupid and I won't pretend that it's okay.

For the record, I myself have ADHD.

CHAPTER 6: OVERMEDICATING OUR YOUTH

"The fastest-growing drug problem in the United States isn't cocaine, heroin, or methamphetamines. It is prescription drugs, and it is profoundly affecting the lives of teenagers." — U.S. Department of Health & Human Services

So, we've got a young person from a broken home who lacks self esteem and carries around a bunch of other baggage as a result of a stressful home life, who then gets bullied early in school because of his timid and seclusive demeanor, whose parents now feel he should be medicated with psychotropic drugs at the request of his teacher along with confirmation of that from a doctor, because — well, they're the "experts", right?

HOW THE HUMAN BRAIN DEVELOPS

The average baby's brain doubles in size in the first year after birth. It grows to about 80% of an adult's size by age 3 and then to 90% in size — nearly full grown — by age 5.[82] The human brain pretty much completes maturing in physical size during adolescence. But critical developments within regions of the brain continue to take place well into a person's twenties.[83]

| *...critical developments within regions of the brain continue to take place well into one's 20's.* |

The development of the prefrontal cortex, a very significant part of the brain in terms of social interactions, is blossoming all during a young person's life. The prefrontal cortex affects how we regulate emotions, control impulsive behavior, assess risk, and make long-term plans.[84] More specifically, the orbital cortex — the part of the prefrontal cortex located just above the eye sockets — and the ventromedial prefrontal cortex is also continuing to develop during this time. This area of the brain controls inhibition, social behavior, ethics, and morality.[85]

Have you ever wondered why children are so impulsive and can make such bad decisions at times? Well, the reason is pretty simple considering their brains are still years aways from maturing in these critical decision making areas. Again, while a young person's brain may be physically mature in size, it is absolutely in its primordial stages of development both naturally and with direct input from their immediate environment early in life. Disorders involving aggression have been linked to dysfunction in these areas of the brain[86] noting a possible link to its early stages of development.

HOW THE HUMAN BRAIN COMMUNICATES WITH THE BODY

The human brain communicates with the body by sending messages via chemical substances called *neurotransmitters* that are many times dictating simple tasks like breathing as well as much more complex tasks such as moods.[87] These neurotransmitters are distributed throughout the brain along pathways calls *synapses* that deliver these messages - the neurotransmitters — between *neurons*. These neurons essentially take these messages and process them accordingly.

For the sake of simplification (it's not you, it's me!), let's look at this process like a mailman delivering really important packages. The neurotransmitters are the *packages*, the synapses are the *roads* the mailman drives on to deliver the packages, and the neurons are the *homes* waiting on the packages to arrive before doing something with them. But things don't always go as planned regarding this scenario.

| *The inability of neurons to properly communicate with one another...can lead to depression.* |

Imagine if some of these homes (neurons) don't communicate very well with one another regarding some very important issues (neurotransmitters) because there are several obstacles in the middle of the roads (synapses) between Home A (neuron) and Home B (neuron). So the packages (neurotransmitters) are not being delivered properly regardless of how well the mailman is attempting to deliver them along our roads (synapses). The inability of these homes (neurons) to properly communicate with one another is called "synaptic plasticity" and can lead to depression, among other things, in people of all ages.

For the purpose of this book we'll focus on two of these very important neurotransmitters (packages) that process information in our brains that are directly affected by mood altering drugs. These neurotransmitters are *serotonin* and *dopamine*.

WHY MOOD ALTERING DRUGS ARE PRESCRIBED

Serotonin is a key neurotransmitter (package) in the brain that is best known for its role in digestion, sexual function, and emotion. It's a pretty big deal in the pecking order of neurotransmitters. When serotonin levels are ideal in the human body we tend to have much more stable moods because it (the package) is delivered properly to the appropriate neurons (homes). However, lower levels of serotonin have been associated with depression and anxiety as well as many other psychological conditions. So, how do we manage serotonin levels in the brain?

Selective serotonin reuptake inhibitors (SSRIs) are a class of drugs that are typically used to treat these particular conditions. We'll call these drugs our *bridges* over the obstacles in the roads (synapses) for the sake of my elementary approach. These SSRIs block or slow the *reuptake* (reabsorption) of serotonin in the brain allowing for higher amounts of serotonin to be utilized. Prozac (fluoxetine) is one of the many SSRIs[88] (bridges) whose function is to increase the concentration of serotonin in the synapses (roads). And in many cases of people with depression and anxiety it does an incredible job. This would be awesome if that's all that took place when serotonin levels were elevated. However, sometimes *bridges* have defects.

WHAT COULD GO WRONG?

Let's look at another very important neurotransmitter in the brain called *dopamine*. Dopamine is a neurotransmitter (package) that is best known for its role in pleasure and motivation. When dopamine levels are ideal, it rewards us with a sense of pleasure and accomplishment whenever we achieve something. But according to the National Institute of Mental Health, too little dopamine — or problems in the way the brain uses dopamine — may play a major role in disorders such as schizophrenia or attention deficit hyperactivity disorder (ADHD). So, why does that matter?

| *Researchers know that these drugs also produce profound, long-lasting, functional alterations in the brain.* |

Researchers have discovered that some SSRIs like Prozac may not just serve their intended purpose to improve levels of serotonin in the brain, but they may also inadvertently redirect dopamine signaling by "tricking" transporters of dopamine into uptake of serotonin instead. This may cause "co-signaling" and lower amounts of dopamine which can, in turn, induce depressive symptoms. Since serotonin plays such a vital role in neuronal development, disruption by Prozac (fluoxetine) of the normal serotonin as well as dopamine levels during development may be responsible for such unusual behavioral abnormalities.[89] There's irrefutable evidence that exists linking these same drugs to pathological side effects of varying degrees of severity. Researchers know that these drugs also produce profound, long-lasting, functional alterations in the brain.[90]

I ran across a study in the *American Journal of Psychiatry* of patients who were suffering from depression — but free of any recent serious suicidal ideation — who were given fluoxetine (Prozac) for treatment. In as little as 2 weeks and as many as 7, six patients developed "intense, preoccupation with violent suicide". All six patients were immediately removed from the medication, but the preoccupation with suicide lasted for as many as 3 months in some cases.[91]

Over 28 million people have taken Prozac and other related antidepressant drugs such as Zoloft, Paxil, and Luvox, and most of these people experience positive results. But in many young people, the "overstimulation reaction" we discussed has been linked to compulsive thoughts of suicide and violence which shockingly occurs in an estimated 1% to 3% of patients.[92] That's 280,000 people — using the smaller number of 1% — running around with suicidal and violent thoughts provoked by taking these prescribed medications.

Let's not forget that all of these types of medications, along with amphetamines and methylphenidates used to treat ADHD, have "black box warnings" — *the most severe warning from the FDA* — that alert the public and health care providers of serious side effects such as suicidal or homicidal thoughts, injury, or death.

Now, like all the other disclaimers found throughout this book, I'm not implying that every young person who takes a psychotropic drug will turn out to be a rampage killer. The data and findings are simply being disseminated for people to have all available information that they may not otherwise be being told.

BRAIN DEVELOPMENT CAN BE ALTERED BY MEDICATIONS

According to the Substance Abuse and Mental Health Services Administration (SAMHSA)[93], the impact of prescription drugs can be particularly disruptive and harmful to a developing child's brain and body. In almost every instance the dosage and indication for psychotropic medications are based on extrapolated adult data, which are not always appropriate for very young children, school-age prepubertal children, or adolescents.[94]

| This means that children on antidepressants could be trading one psychiatric diagnosis for another, all the while permanently altering the brain's long term growth. |

Some studies have found that SSRIs can interfere with normal growth patterns in children's still-developing brains. This means that children on antidepressants could be trading one psychiatric diagnosis for another, all the while permanently altering the brain's long term growth.

ARE TEACHERS QUALIFIED TO RECOMMEND MEDICATION?

Generally speaking, education professionals are trained in education, not medicine. So when they make recommendations to treat a child with medication of anything short of an aspirin for a headache, they are not only in way over their heads, but they are bordering on practicing medicine without a license. Regardless, many teachers routinely tell parents when their children should begin taking medication and even go so far as to tell them what they should prescribe them.[95] I cannot begin to explain how dangerous this is. Being around lots of children taking psychotropic drugs doesn't qualify teachers to prescribe medication to children any more than me being around a bunch of teachers qualifies me to teach.

The point here is not that educators shouldn't have any input regarding children they teach if there are some deficiencies and the child is struggling, but they should be detailing a potential problem so that actual experts in their respective fields can make accurate recommendations based on that feedback.

Medications should be viewed as *one* of the many tools in a toolbox to assist struggling children, not the *only* one. It should never be the "go-to" every time a child is difficult to teach or struggling. Additional tools in the toolbox other than medicinal methods include education and skills training for the child and family, strategies for understanding and building your child's social skills, and classroom management strategies/study skills. If you go straight to medication for your child, you are being just as irresponsible as the teacher incorrectly recommending it.

But all doctors are right — right?

ARE ALL DOCTORS QUALIFIED TO PRESCRIBE ALL MEDICATIONS?

In a study between 1995 and 2007, almost 1 in 10 visits to *primary care physicians* resulted in the patient coming away with a prescription for an antidepressant. But in only 44% of these cases did the doctor make a formal diagnosis of major depression or anxiety disorder properly justifying the prescription. During this time, both primary care physicians and specialists drastically stepped up their prescribing of antidepressants. Even as they did so, fewer and fewer of the patients who got those prescriptions got a psychiatric diagnosis along with their pills.[96]

> | *The number of U.S. preschoolers diagnosed with attention-deficit hyperactivity disorder (ADHD) jumped 56% between 2007 and 2012...* |

And we're not just talking about teenagers being prescribed these mood altering drugs. The number of U.S. preschoolers diagnosed with attention-deficit hyperactivity disorder (ADHD) jumped 56% between 2007 and 2012 and the number of children ages 2 to 5 taking a psychoactive medication to treat ADHD doubled.[97]

It's important that we understand that psychotropic medication is not some universal "fix" that makes a student's learning or behavior challenges disappear. Even in the best of circumstances — when medication helps reduce symptoms — it does not solve the underlying problems.[98] Masking the problem itself does nothing to "fix" it. And by pushing medication first onto our children at such a young age, we're not only conditioning them to consider medication a quick and easy solution rather than trying other methods of treatment, but we're also rewiring the child's brain as it develops.

There are 28 million people who have taken Prozac and other related antidepressant drugs such as Zoloft, Paxil, and Luvox, which are thought to increase levels of serotonin. Of these, about 70% get their prescriptions — *not psychiatrists* — from primary care physicians who often have neither the time nor the necessary expertise to fully evaluate their patients' mental health and advise them about different therapies. Many primary care doctors aren't happy with this state of affairs, but they feel pressured by health insurers not to refer patients to specialists.[99]

Clearly SSRIs and other mood-altering drugs can serve a significant purpose in helping many people cope with the psychological challenges they face. These drugs have proven effective in providing many people the tools necessary to face otherwise daunting challenges and obstacles in their lives. But it would be willfully ignorant of us as a society to ignore the potential negative effects these medications can have on some individuals.

WHAT MEDICATIONS CAN HAVE NEGATIVE EFFECTS PER THE FDA?

A 2010 study of all serious adverse event reports for drugs with 200 or more cases received from 2004 through September 2009 found that of the 31 drugs disproportionately associated with violence (out of 484 available drugs), they accounted for 79% (1,527 of 1,937) of the violence cases reported.[100] Of the drugs identified were a smoking cessation aid, 11 antidepressant drugs, 3 drugs for attention deficit hyperactivity disorder, and 5 hypnotic/sedatives.[101]

Here's a table with the 31 drugs associated with violence. Keep in mind that this data for violent cases came directly from the Food and Drug Administration (FDA) Adverse Event Reporting System (AERS).

Drug Name	Violence Cases
VARENICLINE	408
FLUOXETINE	72
PAROXETINE	177
AMPHETAMINES	31
MEFLOQUINE	10
ATOMOXETINE	50
TRIAZOLAM	7
FLUVOXAMINE	5
VENLAFAXINE	85
DESVENLAFAXINE	8
MONTELUKAST	53
SERTRALINE	64
ZOLPIDEM	48
ESCITALOPRAM	31
SODIUM OXYBATE	6
CITALOPRAM	34
ARIPIPRAZOLE	23
OXYCODONE	46
BUPROPION	35

ZIPRASIDONE	19
METHYLPHENIDATE	27
MIRTAZAPINE	15
GABAPENTIN	35
LEVETIRACETAM	21
DIAZEPAM	11
ALPRAZOLAM	15
DULOXETINE	45
CLONAZEPAM	10
INTERFERON ALFA	54
RISPERIDONE	29
QUETIAPINE	53

There were no violence cases reported for the other 324 evaluable drugs out of the available 484 (66.9%) and 1 or 2 cases were reported for an additional 86 of the available 484 (17.8%) evaluable drugs. On the other hand, 84.7% of all evaluable drugs in widespread clinical use did not appear to be associated with violence.[102]

Maybe it's just odd timing, but the massive spike in children being prescribed these drugs at such an early age began right smack in the middle of No Child Left Behind. Weird, right?

CHAPTER 7: THE DEVIL'S TRIANGLE

"...feeling pleasure in the face of other people's pain is essential to evil character."[103] — *Todd Calder*

So far we've taken a quick trip through the topics of broken homes, bullied youth, and medicated youth. As you've seen, these are by far three of the most common denominators found in rampage killers. Sure there are other less common causal factors that many of these killers share (see Chapter 14), but I couldn't find any others that were as common in nearly all instances or as psychologically impactful. And these three can produce some pretty dark results if not properly managed.

Let's pluck just one statistic from each of the three main causal factors that I list in the book to establish the case for these being the most common and important causal factors regarding rampage killers:

- 75% of the most notorious "school killers" in recent history were raised in broken homes.[104]

- Nearly 75% of "school killings" have been linked to harassment and bullying.[105]

- 90% of "school shootings" for over a decade were linked directly to SSRI antidepressants like Prozac, Paxil, and

Zoloft.[106] Of the 31 drugs disproportionately associated with violence, they account for 79% of all violence cases.[107]

This is clear cut event correlation as described in Chapter 2: Root Cause Analysis. These constantly occurring commonalities regarding rampage killers is undeniable.

| ***...one can have all the symptoms of a disease and not have the disease.*** |

An obvious question — and a fair one to ask — is that if I'm so sure these three factors have such an influence on rampage killers, why aren't all or most people from broken homes who are bullied and on psychotropic medication transformed into rampage killers as a result? Well, it's like any other physical or mental ailment if you ask any physician — *a person can have all the symptoms of a disease and not have the disease.* For example, my mother smoked cigarettes for 50 or so years from what I can remember. She probably even smoked when she was pregnant with me, which would explain a lot. (Times were different in the 1960's!) But while my mom had most symptoms and ailments associated with patients diagnosed with lung cancer, she never had the slightest issue relating to lung cancer or cancer of any kind.

So, if my mother smoked potentially cancer-causing cigarettes for 50 years and never contracted cancer, are the warning labels on the sides of packs of cigarettes wrong?

No, of course not. Smoking cigarettes *can* cause cancer just like being from a broken home, being bullied, and taking mood altering drugs *can* help produce a rampage killer. And of course not all rampage killers will have all three of these traits just like some people who die of lung cancer have never smoked a cigarette their entire lives.

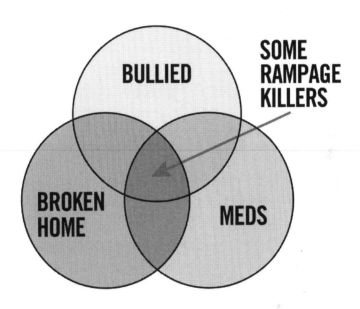

THE 5 WHYS OF DETERMINING ROOT CAUSE IN RAMPAGE KILLERS

In Chapter 2 we discussed the 5 whys of determining a root cause analysis. After 2 quick whys we proved in the simplest of ways that firearms were definitely not the root cause of rampage killers. But what is? Let's do a more thorough run through of the exercise:

FIRST WHY: "Why is that person dead?"
ANSWER: "He was shot with a firearm."

SECOND WHY: "Why was he shot with a firearm?"
ANSWER: "The killer was upset/angry."

THIRD WHY: "Why was he upset/angry?"
ANSWER: "He was bullied and ostracized at school."

FOURTH WHY: "Why was he bullied and ostracized at school?"
ANSWER: "He had awkward social skills and was a loner."

FIFTH WHY: "Why did he have awkward social skills and was a loner?"
ANSWER: "He had low self esteem and self confidence."

SIXTH WHY: "Why did he have low self esteem and self confidence?"
ANSWER: "He was devalued by a seldom present parent."

SEVENTH WHY: "Why was he devalued by a seldom present parent?"
ANSWER:

Without the parent's involvement at this point, it's tough to continue with the whys. But there is a subset of whys to be asked:

EIGHTH WHY: "As many as 90% of some kids are bullied and they don't kill people. Why did this guy?"

ANSWER: "He was on an SSRI medication that causes depression, irritability, suicidal and homicidal thoughts, and aggression and then he stopped taking his medication and withdrawal symptoms exacerbated his condition."

NINTH WHY: "Many young people are on those medications that never choose to kill people. Why did this guy?"

ANSWER: "Maybe genetics?"

So, after 9 whys, we've determined that our rampage killer had potential genetic abnormalities, was from a broken home, was bullied, and was medicated.

THE DOMINO EFFECT

As evidenced by the "5 whys" exercise above, the causal factors I've focused on appear to have a direct impact on each other. I mention in Chapter 1 that sociopaths have some genetic predispositions that are then impacted or triggered by environmental influencers. Many of these young people end up becoming loners and act more socially awkward than their peers as a result of the lack of self esteem, trust issues, rejection issues, loneliness, etc. that come from living in a broken home. They're then bullied, ostracized, and made fun of as a result of those actions. As a result of *that*, many of these children end up being medically treated for various conditions like anxiety and depression. Let's remind ourselves that at times these treatments consist of medications that intensify and worsen the child's mental state, especially when they stop taking them and begin to withdraw.

To deny that a broken home or childhood trauma can be a precursor to a kid being bullied which can then be a precursor to a kid needing medication to cope is just being dishonest with the facts available to us. In many cases, being raised in a home that isn't broken would produce a socially functional young person with confidence and self esteem making it very unlikely they'd need to be medicated to cope with their emotions. So the child never enters into the "devil's triangle" where we have to cross our fingers that they don't become suicidal or homicidal. And if the kid does come from a broken home and still manages to overcome that and be socially accepted (like so many do), again, it's more likely there won't be feelings of depression or anxiety that need to be medicated.

One thing is for sure, though — while nearly all rampage killers have had all 3 of the factors I point out, absolutely every single one of them had, at the very least, two of them. These factors aren't coincidences like if half of them liked Metallica and also vanilla ice cream or something arbitrary. Being from a broken home, bullied, and medicated with psychotropic drugs are commonalities that directly shape personalities.

But let's not lose sight of the millions of children who come from perfectly good homes who are not bullied and who are still placed on psychotropic drugs as a result of them having ADHD. Those drugs alone can produce suicidal and homicidal ideation without any other stressors or causal factors. For that reason, parents should still be fully aware of the associated negative side effects of these medications.

Again, most people who possess the three causal factors I highlight are *not* rampage killers. But — *some are*.

Chapter 8: SEUNG-HUI CHO - VIRGINIA TECH

"Oh the happiness I could have had mingling among you hedonists, being counted as one of you, only if you didn't fuck the living shit out of me.

You could have been great. I could have been great. Ask yourself what you did to me to have made me clean the slate." - from Sueng-Hui Cho's manifesto

At 5:00 a.m. on April 16, 2007, one of Sueng-Hui Cho's Virginian Tech college roommates sees Cho awake at his computer. Shortly after that, one of his other roommates sees him brushing his teeth and putting acne cream on his face. Cho then finishes getting dressed and leaves for the day. Four hours and twenty-one minutes later, after firing 174 rounds, killing 32 people, and wounding another 17, Sueng-Hui Cho shoots himself in the head, ending his life.

The Virginia Tech killings were carried out with two handguns and remains one of the worst rampage killings in America.

BROKEN HOME

Just like a family's journey from South Korea to the United States is somewhat nontraditional, Cho's family's broken home was pretty nontraditional. Cho's mother, Hyang-Im

Cho, was forced into an arranged marriage to his father, Sung-Tae Cho, who was ten years older than her. At 29 years old, Hyang-Im was relatively old for an unmarried South Korean woman and her father forced her to accept the proposal from the older Sung-Tae Cho. Hyang-Im wasn't interested in him, but she reluctantly agreed to the marriage under the circumstances. Hyang-Im's aunt, Yong-Soon, once said regarding the marriage, "Her husband was not fit for her. But she always followed and obeyed him." It was a marriage built on convenience and tradition, not love.

| *The younger Cho never spoke highly of his father.* |

Barely making ends meet, both of Cho's parents worked at dry cleaners nearly all the time. Even when Mr. Cho was around, he didn't have many pleasant conversations with his son. The younger Cho struggled his entire life with speech and speaking clearly where others could understand him. While Mr. Cho was somewhat tolerant of his son's unwillingness to speak, he stood very firm on traditional matters and being respectful of others. Mr. Cho felt his son showed disrespect to others by not answering when spoken to or refusing to have conversations with those who attempted to communicate with him. The two had heated disagreements concerning this.[108] The younger Cho never spoke highly of his father.

In South Korean culture, the model of the man as the breadwinner along with most parents pushing their children to be more educated and prosperous than themselves certainly put additional pressure on an already struggling Seuing-Hui Cho. His older sister, Sun-Kyung, was offered full ride scholarships to both Harvard and Princeton, settling on the latter, and was excelling at everything she did. Meanwhile, Seuing-Hui became more and more withdrawn and isolated in everything he did. This only added to Mr. Cho's disappointment in his son.

BULLIED

According to assistant professor of sociology and criminology at Adelphi University, Jessie Klein, "Cho's family, roommates, teachers, professors and judges all recognized that he needed help. They knew he was bullied, and they saw that he was miserable and angry..."[109]

Whether he was angry about the bullying or simply ashamed of it, Cho wouldn't openly discuss the bullying. His sister mentioned at times that students would yell various insults at him in the hallways at school. He didn't talk about his feelings or problems at school at all. If asked how things were going, Cho would simply respond, "okay". Things were certainly not "okay" with Cho. Something was building up inside him that no one could have predicted.

| *As soon as he started reading, the whole class started laughing and pointing and saying, 'Go back to China.* |

There was one time where Cho's English teacher had students reading aloud to the class. When it became was Cho's turn to read, he kept his head down and would not look up. The teacher pressed him to read. After several requests for Cho to read, his teacher threatened to give him a failing grade if he did not. So Cho read. It only made things worse. One of the other students in his class later reported that when he finally started reading, his voice had a strange, deep sound and sounded "like he had something in his mouth. As soon as he started reading, the whole class started laughing and pointing and saying, 'Go back to China.'"[110] I'd like to point out that this is an incredibly poorly thought-out strategy by this teacher. This is a perfect example of teachers participating in bullying. I'm sure this teacher's class thought she was super cool with how she handled the situation. I'm sure her street credentials were boosted nicely with the eruption of laughter at Mr. Cho's expense. But make no mistake, this is a classic example of bullying by authority and this teacher did nothing but contribute to the atrocities that Cho would go on to commit.

Some people thought Cho was mute because he spoke so little. Along with his depression, he was diagnosed with "selective mutism", a mental condition where the patient chooses not to speak. Imagine being so self-conscious of your poor speech that you never speak out loud for fear of being picked on and made fun of because of it.

Looking for any way to help her son's noticeable downward spiral, Cho's mother attempted to get him involved in her church at one point. She was a very religious person and was intent on trying to make things better for Cho. But no sooner had Cho joined the Bible study group there than some of the "rich" kids in his class began to bully him. This went on for as long as Cho attended the group sessions. Clearly this bullying at church had a staying effect on Cho as evidenced by this passage from his manifesto: *"All of you who have ever been fucked by these Descendants of Satan Disguised as Devout Christians, all of you who have went through what I went through, all of you who have felt what I have felt in my life, all of you who have suffered the wrath of these Democratic Terrorists, all of you who have been beaten, humiliated, and crucified* — "[111]

MEDICATED

It still amazes me how many "experts" either ignore facts in their respective fields or are purposefully deceptive. When medical records were finally released for Sueng-Hui Cho, Doug Rollins, a toxicologist at the Center for Human Toxicology at the University of Utah stated, "I would say that drugs probably did not play a role in his actions on that particular day. Most of those drugs, once they're not in the bloodstream, they're not having a pharmacological effect."[112] Mr. Rollins made sure to say *probably* and *most*, because he clearly wasn't certain if drugs played a role in Cho's actions and he surely knew that many drugs do not need to be in the bloodstream in order to affect the patient.

In 2003, British officials warned doctors against prescribing Paxil — the antidepressant Cho had been taking — for depression in children and teens. The statement from the U.K.'s Medicines and Healthcare products Regulatory Agency stated *"It has become clear that the benefits of [Paxil] in children for the treatment of depressive illness do not outweigh these risks."* The risks being a potentially worsening mental state. But in spite of overwhelming evidence, U.S. officials at the FDA said at the time that they had not yet decided whether to issue a similar warning. This was after Paxil manufacturer GlaxoSmithKline released a report of more than 1,000 pediatric patients taking Paxil for depression where it was determined that suicidal thoughts and attempts were twice as high among children and adolescents taking Paxil than among those taking placebos .[113]

Many of these aforementioned SSRIs have more serious side affects — like suicidal thoughts and activation of mania[114] — once the prescribed patient stops taking the medications. Cho had been prescribed Prozac and took it for some time, but then stopped. Prozac's very own FDA-mandated black box warning label states "Increased risk of suicidal thinking and behavior in children, adolescents, and young adults taking antidepressants for Major Depressive Disorder (MDD) and other psychiatric disorders."[115] Mr. Rollins chose to ignore these facts or simply wasn't aware of them. However, I'm no toxicologist and even I'm aware of this. Instances like this are particularly why people have so little faith in so many of today's "experts" because although most data and information is readily available to anyone with moderate intelligence to research and read, so many "experts" who know better — or should — give out inconsistent and incorrect information.

A DIFFERENT KIND OF BROKEN, BUT BROKEN NONETHELESS

Cho's home issues were certainly different from those of most rampage killers. But the commonalities that tie him to this group are further proof that even strict cultural traditions and standards sometimes can't overcome these powerful causal effects. I see Cho's home as broken based on the lack of true love that accompanies a "planned marriage" and the fact that his father was not only rarely around, but that he was open about his disappointment in his son in a culture where the man is the primary bread winner of the family and the top of the familial hierarchy. These things, along with Cho's poor speech and depression, led him to be bullied all throughout school and even at church. Was Cho then medicated because of depression associated with a broken home or from being bullied? Only Cho could've answered that, but clearly all of these issues bundled together had proven to be too overwhelming.

Chapter 9: ERIC HARRIS - COLUMBINE HIGH SCHOOL

"I hate you people for leaving me out of so many fun things. And no don't ... say, 'Well that's your fault,' because it isn't, you people had my phone #, and I asked and all, but no. No no no don't let the weird-looking Eric KID come along." - an Eric Harris journal entry

It was the morning of Tuesday, April 20, 1999. Columbine High School students, Eric Harris and Dylan Klebold, carefully and methodically positioned a homemade bomb in an area nearby Columbine High School that was meant to detonate at 11:14 a.m. as a diversion from the school where the two would be teenage killers would be carrying out their attack on students and faculty.

Moments later at Columbine High School, Rachel Scott and Richard Castaldo were the first to be hunted down on campus and shot. Eric fired his gun into Richard's arms and torso and Rachel was shot in the chest and head. Rachel was killed instantly. Richard played dead, saving his life.[116]

At 12:08 p.m., Harris and Klebold returned to the school's library they'd exited a few minutes earlier where they'd taunted and terrorized 56 students and faculty and now decided to end the rampage by taking their own lives. After killing 12 people and injuring 26, Harris and Klebold chose to take the sociopath coward's common way out where both died of self inflicted gunshots to the head.[117]

|...the Columbine shootings would've been part of a much larger rampage killing if things had gone his way... "

According to writings from Harris, the Columbine shootings would've been part of a much larger rampage killing if things had gone his way. Their intent was to blow up the better part of Columbine High School with the two propane bombs they'd built and placed in the cafeteria at the school just prior to the killings. Had those bombs properly detonated, they would've most likely killed the more than 400 people in the cafeteria during the "A" period lunch break and also collapsed the cafeteria ceiling with the library being directly above it. Harris had planned to continue their rampage into the adjoining areas of town near the school — killing as many people as they could — and then even highjacking an airplane and flying it to New York City where they would crash it.

|...picture half of (D)enver on fire just from me and Vodka (Klebold)...|

Further proof that the Columbine cafeteria and library weren't the killers' only targets can be found in one of Harris' journal entries on October 23, 1998 that read:

"God I want to torch and level everything in this whole fucking area but Bombs of that size are hard to make, and plus I would need a fuckin fully loaded A-10 to get every store on wadsworth and all the buildings downtown. heh, Imagine THAT ya fuckers, picture half of denver on fire just from me and Vodka (Klebold). napalm on sides of skyscrapers and car garages blowing up from exploded gas tanks.... oh man that would be beautiful."[118]

The homemade propane fueled bombs in the cafeteria and offsite never detonated as planned.

THE SOCIOPATH LEADS THE FOLLOWER

Based on a history of actions and comments by both Harris and Klebold, it's obvious that both boys were not sociopaths. Harris definitely was one and he was clearly the leader of the two. He was proudly deceitful and often had a tendency to be violent and aggressive, as noted by many of his schoolmates. Once a friend and neighbor refused to continue giving Harris a ride to school at which point Harris reacted by breaking the windshield on the teen's car by throwing a heavy object through it. This even got the attention of Harris' father at this point in time as he himself began to keep a log of his son's misdeeds going forward.

But Klebold was simply a sad, depressed, suicidal boy crying out for help. Harris — purposely or unintentionally — took advantage of Klebold's tendency to follow him. Validating this point, a team of psychiatrists later noted in a

2004 published article that Klebold "...would never have pulled off Columbine without Harris. He might have gotten caught for some petty crime, gotten help in the process, and conceivably could have gone on to live a normal life."[119] It's sad and unfortunate that his parents couldn't spot Klebold's obvious depression along with the boy's need to be accepted among his peers. Couple this with the fact that he was engaged with weapons acquisition and bomb making and it makes me wonder how all of this managed to fly under the radar until the deadly murders took place.

And clearly this book should've come along sooner — for many reasons — but Harris evidently had himself confused with a psychopath as evidenced by this entry to his and Klebold's "Basement Tapes" recordings where he stated:

"My parents are the best fucking parents I have ever known. My dad is great. I wish I was a fucking sociopath so I didn't have any remorse, but I do. This is going to tear them apart. They will never forget it. There is nothing you guys could have done to prevent any of this. There is nothing that anyone could have done to prevent this. No one is to blame except me and Vodka (Klebold). Our actions are a two man war against everyone else."

Harris did not openly appear to have issues at home.

BROKEN HOME

Eric Harris is one of the few examples I use in this book who appear to have the *least* broken home out of all of rampage killers. Harris' dad, Wayne Harris, was stationed at six different Air Force bases across the country in Eric Harris' first twelve years of life before settling in Colorado as a result of a forced retirement due to government cutbacks. While Mr. Harris did live with his family, clearly his job was a high priority to him. Is it possible the constant moving took its toll with Harris always having to start over with making friends? I recall that when I was a boy, our family moved once to a new school district and it was very hard on us kids. We lost every friend and went to a school where we knew no one. Imagine doing that six times before eighth grade.

> **"...(authorities) found explosive devices, gunpowder and the sawed-off barrel of the shotgun Harris used in the massacre..."**[120]

One other indicator that Mr. and Mrs. Harris may not have been all that present in Eric's life is the fact that when authorities searched Eric Harris' bedroom after the event, they found explosive devices, gunpowder and the sawed-off barrel of the shotgun Harris used in the massacre.[121] I do my best not to judge other parents because we all have our own challenges when it comes to parenting. But I'd be remiss not to mention how uninvolved a parent has to be in their child's life not to notice the procurement of firearms and explosives that are being stored under the same roof you live under and pay the mortgage for. I'm maybe slightly more engaged with my own son than that. But who am I to judge?

BULLIED

As I stated in Chapter 4, many times teachers and administrators not only look the other way regarding bullying in schools, sometimes they too take part in it. Sure, that's a hard pill to swallow, especially for those it incriminates. But it would appear that Columbine High School principal, Frank DeAngelis, is either protecting the school's participation in bullying Harris and Klebold or just trying to avoid the fact that they allowed it to happen. Mr. DeAngelis stated in an October 3, 2020 Denver Post article that "stories of a Columbine jock culture prone to bullying kids like Harris and Klebold was a myth, that there was no Trenchcoat Mafia and that staff members didn't detect bullying or have any warning of what was to happen."[122]

Let's see, I count at least two outright lies from Mr. DeAngelis. Sure, it's possible that staff members were too stupid and ignorant to see the rampant bullying that took place at Columbine High School, but it's very unlikely. In fact, several witnesses in a massive lawsuit against the school district, sheriff's office, and the parents of the two killers, stated that "bullying was a daily phenomenon and that school administrators, including DeAngelis, ignored it."[123] Additionally, there was absolutely a Trenchcoat Mafia. I'm not even going to waste my time referencing that with an endnote as it's not only common knowledge, but it's also referenced by Harris and Klebold as well as by other students. It's possible Mr. DeAngelis was the only one not aware of this clique in his school, which makes me question any of his other statements about the school since it's clear he was not involved in the its daily actions enough to acknowledge this popular group of outcasts.

| *"That happened while teachers watched."* *- An incident of Harris and Klebold being bullied.* |

Classmates and parents gave many reports of the bullying of the two killers with one classmate describing one horrifying incident, stating that students had surrounded Harris and Klebold in the commons and thrown ketchup-covered tampons at them, laughing and calling them faggots.[124] One student stated, "That happened while teachers watched. They couldn't fight back. They wore the ketchup all day and went home covered with it." Klebold had reportedly stated that this had been the worst day of his life. In a separate incident, the two boys had human feces thrown on them. A myth?

Harris and Klebold were, in fact, bullied so much that nearly every time they posted entries to various journals, made posts online, or filmed various videos, they more times than not exhibited a heightened level of rage for being bullied at the school and openly expressed it.

Harris and Klebold were such outcasts and outsiders at school that they weren't even accepted into the Trenchcoat

Mafia of self-proclaimed outcasts and outsiders who dressed in all-black garb. Harris and Klebold certainly had some friends at school. They were definitely not isolated loners. But sometimes kids long to be accepted by the "cool kids" and these two were not. Princeton sociologist Katherine Newman, says young people such as Harris and Klebold are not loners — that they're just not accepted by the kids *who count*. "Getting attention by becoming notorious is better than being a failure."[125] The kids they sought approval and acceptance from were not going to give it.

MEDICATED

A great deal of effort has gone into attempting to build the narrative that the Luvox (Fluvoxamine) found in Eric Harris' bloodstream during his autopsy had no effect whatsoever on his actions and that SSRIs are completely harmless:

"Jefferson County authorities confirmed Monday that Eric Harris had a psychotropic drug called Luvox in his bloodstream, but an expert said there is no scientific evidence connecting such medication to behavior changes that involve hostile outbursts."[126] - DenverPost.com

"Despite a decade of research, there is little valid evidence to prove a causal relationship between the use of anti-depressant medications and destructive behavior. On the other hand, there is ample evidence that undiagnosed and

untreated mental illness exacts a heavy toll on those who suffer from these disorders, as well as those around them,"[127] *- CNN.com*

But according to the manufacturer, Solvay, this is not true as 4% of young people taking Luvox had developed mania during short-term controlled clinical trials. Mania is a psychosis which can produce bizarre, grandiose, highly elaborated destructive plans, including mass murder.[128] It would appear that the Denver Post and CNN need to step up their research efforts. But don't just take the manufacturer's word for it — or mine. Here's the FDA's own "black box" warning label for Luvox:

*Depression and certain other psychiatric disorders are themselves associated with increases in the **risk of suicide**. Patients with major depressive disorder (MDD), both adult and pediatric, **may experience worsening of their depression and/or the emergence of suicidal ideation** and behavior (suicidality) or unusual changes in behavior, whether or not they are taking antidepressant medications. This risk may persist until significant remission occurs.*

*In short-term studies, **antidepressants increased the risk of suicidality in children, adolescents, and young adults** when compared to placebo. Short-term studies did not show an increase in the risk of suicidality with antidepressants compared to placebo in adults beyond age 24. Adults age 65 and older taking antidepressants have a decreased risk of suicidality. Patients, their families, and caregivers should be alert to the emergence of anxiety, restlessness,* *irritability, aggressiveness and insomnia. If these symptoms emerge, they should be reported to the patient's prescriber or health care professional. All patients being treated with antidepressants for any indication should watch for and notify their health care provider for worsening symptoms, suicidality and unusual changes in behavior, especially during the first few months of treatment.[129]*

I'm still waiting for someone to explain to me how this along with all other anecdotal evidence on the negative side effects of Luvox isn't deemed "scientific evidence" or "valid evidence" by the media.

Chapter 10: ADAM LANZA - SANDY HOOK ELEMENTARY SCHOOL

"I incessantly have nothing other than scorn for humanity. I have been desperate to feel anything positive for someone for my entire life." - Adam Lanza

At 9:30 a.m. on December 14, 2012, to her horror, first grade teacher Lauren Rousseau heard gunshots over the loudspeaker as announcements were being read to the school that morning. A quick-thinking Lauren rounded her sixteen students up in the restroom inside her classroom to hide them from whomever was firing the shots. This act of courage was a more heroic deed than most people will ever have to make in their entire lifetime. Sadly, the killer, Adam Lanza, found the sixteen first graders and Lauren hiding in their last minute shelter. Only one of the children survived his onslaught.

As a father, this rampage killing shook me to the core. At the time of the murders, my own son was near the same age as most of the children murdered. I remember barely being able to eat that evening as I looked at my son and played out the scenario at Sandy Hook Elementary in my head as if it were happening at my own son's school. I imagined the emotional tsunami that twenty other fathers just like me were going through that very night. I couldn't take my eyes off of my son that night. I slept most of the night with him in his bed even after he'd fallen asleep.

BROKEN HOME

Adam Lanza's father, Peter Lanza, had himself grown up in a home where his own mother and father were very distant in their relationship and his father very much committed himself to his work and not his family. This was Peter Lanza's only model for being a husband and a father. Like his father before him, Peter immersed himself in his own job as a high ranking accountant at General Electric.[130] He was pretty much absent from home life during the week, but made time to spend with his two sons, Ryan and Adam, on the weekends. This relieved Nancy Lanza, who tended to the boys all week, to run errands and have a bit of a break. Although Peter and Nancy did their best under the circumstances to provide a cohesive family unit, it was not one. The two had drifted apart. They officially separated in 2001 and made it official in 2009 when they divorced. Adam Lanza was nine years old when his parents divorced, but he'd never really experienced any real semblance of what a fundamental family unit is meant to be up to that point.

According to Peter Lanza, Adam and his older son, Ryan (four years Adam's senior), were close early in their lives. Peter said the boys would "spend hours playing at two Lego tables in the basement, making up stories for the little towns they built".[131] But the boys soon drifted apart. By the time Ryan left for college when Adam was fourteen, the boys had a very distant relationship. At the time of the murders, both Ryan and Peter Lanza had not spoken to Adam in over a year.[132]

At age 6, Adam Lanza had been diagnosed with *sensory integration disorder*,[133] a condition where "the brain has trouble organizing and responding to information from the senses". In Adam's case, he had what can be described as "sensory overload" where loud sounds, textures of clothing, and even textures of foods emotionally overwhelmed him. Sensory integration disorder can be genetic and possibly a result of birth complications and other environmental factors.[134]

Nancy Lanza gave up her career as a stockbroker and shaped her own life around her son's various conditions and quirky behaviors in an attempt to satisfy these inadequacies rather than seeking any legitimate outside help for him. One report stated that Nancy Lanza "had sought to appease her son and was inclined to accommodate his disabilities rather than treat them".[135] At times she did laundry for Adam several times a day due to his incessant changing of his socks, sometimes as much as twenty times a day. Nancy made black and white photocopies of Adam's textbooks because their color pages overstimulated his senses. She also caved to his desire to be isolated by pulling him from school permanently and allowing him to disconnect himself from the outside world by staying in his room with little to no in-person contact with anyone, including her. She only communicated with him by talking through the wall that separated their bedrooms or via email. Even when Adam was in ninth grade and Nancy Lanza finally contacted Yale University's Child Study Center because his conditions had gotten so bad, she then ignored all the recommendations by the very people she had sought help from.[136]

About a week before the Sandy Hook Elementary School murders, Nancy Lanza reportedly told a friend, "I'm worried I'm losing him."[137]

BULLIED

One result of Adam Lanza's sensory issues was the fact that he couldn't stand the textures of any food that his mother or anyone else cooked. As a result, his weight was well below that of a healthy young man of his age. At the time of his autopsy, Lanza was 6 feet tall and weighed only 112 pounds. He was clinically anorexic. (It's also worth noting that malnutrition can contribute to brain damage and cognitive impairment.)

Lanza also had a serious speech delay early in life and had trouble communicating. When he was younger, people were constantly asking Adam to repeat himself and this was a source of immense frustration with him. Kids can be cruel and unforgiving. I'm guessing Lanza's communication issues resulted in a few cruel jokes at his expense.

When Nancy Lanza finally removed her son for good from school in his mid-teens, she reportedly told an acquaintance it was after being "not excessively" bullied for his social awkwardness and low weight.[138] Clearly Lanza had mentioned something to his mom about being made fun of at school for her to decide to remove him from that corrosive environment.

MEDICATED

Reports that Lanza's psychiatric issues were "completely untreated in the years before the shooting" are false.[139] Lanza had not only received therapeutic treatment for communication and sensory issues as early as three years old, but when he was fourteen had been prescribed — and took — an antidepressant Celexa or Lexapro (reports vary). Both of these antidepressants are part of the SSRI family and are prescribed for symptoms of major depressive disorder and generalized anxiety disorder.

Reports vary as to how long Lanza took the prescribed medication. And due to sealed records and other obstacles, I was not able to confirm the length of time with any certainty.

THE MEDIA'S RECKLESS AUTISM MOTIVE

Adam Lanza was diagnosed early as being on the Autism spectrum with Aspergers. Even without any other notorious rampage killers or even serial killers being diagnosed with autism over the years, the media — feeling like they needed to have their "reason" for the killings and a potential front page piece — jumped on the horribly irresponsible and hurtful bandwagon of feeling like they'd solved the puzzle by claiming autism was the cause of the killings. This was recklessly stupid. While autism and psychopathy (and sociopathy) can all involve a certain lack of empathy, autistic people typically don't *recognize* physical and verbal cues, so they have trouble interpreting signs and expressing empathy when dealing with others. Psychopaths and sociopaths, however, *do* recognize these cues, they simply don't *care* about others' feelings or if they hurt them.

Adam Lanza methodically planned his rampage killing and knew what he was doing. He misunderstood *nothing* — he simply didn't care. To label him autistic before labeling him a sociopath is careless and dangerous, not to mention just plain ignorant. It would be great if the media devoted even a little time to educating people on autism rather than recklessly throwing around sweeping generalities when they are lost on specific topics.

Chapter 11: NIKOLAS CRUZ - PARKLAND HIGH SCHOOL

"If anything happens to me you know it was Nick."[140]
- Lynda Cruz (Nikolas Cruz's adoptive mother)

At 2:21 p.m. on February 14, 2018, 19 year old Nikolas Cruz entered Building 12 at Marjory Stoneman Douglas High School in Parkland, Florida, — a gun free zone — as he carried a black rifle bag. Within 15 seconds of entry he opened fire into multiple classrooms full of students and faculty.[141]

At 2:28 p.m., Cruz exited the school with evacuating students and faculty, blending in as if he were an innocent bystander. At this time, twelve victims lay dead inside the school building, three more died soon after just outside the building on school grounds, and two more died later after being transported to a hospital.

At 2:32 p.m., four Coral Springs police officers and two Broward County sheriff's deputies entered the building for the first time since the massacre began. This was thirteen minutes after Cruz arrived at the front of the school via an Uber ride.

Flashback to thirteen minutes earlier at 2:19 p.m. when Andrew Medina, a school security monitor, saw Cruz exit the Uber ride he arrived in, he saw him exit the vehicle carrying what he himself identified as a "rifle case", and he saw Cruz enter the school — a "gun free zone" where guns are not allowed — all without any attempt at stopping him OR calling a "code red" on the school radio which would have alerted all other school officials of the potential threat he'd just identified and would've locked down the school.

It's worth noting that a judge in a Broward Circuit Court said that Mr. Medina "acted with reckless indifference" and that the he would be included in a related lawsuit.[142]

BROKEN HOME

Brenda Woodard was a panhandler on various highway and interstate exits and was homeless at frequent times in her adult life. Her criminal record included a 2010 charge for beating her friend with a tire iron as well as a time when she threatened to burn the same friend's house down. Brenda Woodard was also an addict who was arrested for buying crack cocaine while she was pregnant with her son, Nikolas. Brenda was Nikolas Cruz's biological mother.[143]

Nikolas Cruz never knew Brenda Woodard as he was adopted when he was just two days old by Lynda and Roger Cruz. Lynda and Roger Cruz had moved from New York late in life and built a luxurious five-bedroom, three-bath home with a pool in the backyard in sunny Parkland, FL. Lynda was 48 years old and Roger was 61 when they adopted Nikolas. [144]

| *"Nope. Daddy's dead."* |

Mr. Cruz traveled often with his executive marketing job. When Nikolas was just five years old, Lynda Cruz spotted him running down the hallway and then into his room, crying. When she went to try to comfort him and find out why he was upset, she asked "What's the matter, did Daddy punish you?" The five year old Nikolas replied, "Nope. Daddy's dead." Roger Cruz had dropped dead of a massive heart attack in the family's home in front of young Nikolas.[145]

Cruz and his younger brother were raised the remaining years in the home without any father figure present. I'd like to reiterate that children who live in a fatherless home are 279% more likely to carry firearms for offensive purposes compared to children who live with their fathers.[146] This commonality is no coincidence. While poor genes are likely to have contributed to some of Cruz's inadequacies, being raised in a fatherless home is a known statistical risk.

While Cruz's mother was reported to have been good to he and his brother and that she pampered him even more after the elder Cruz passed away[147], Cruz told detectives after the massacre that his parents "put him down" and made him "feel bad"[148]. They also treated his brother the same way. Friends stated that he was "a momma's boy" and that "She was his best friend."[149] Mrs. Cruz passed away three months before the massacre at Marjory Stoneman Douglas.

BULLIED

Nikolas Cruz was an awkward looking high school boy with poor social skills who had few friends and didn't fit in anywhere. He was an outcast. Students openly described his awkwardness and their own alienating of him. If 49% of children in grades 4 through 12 reported being bullied at school as we discussed in a previous chapter,[150] anyone who asserts that they don't think Cruz — with all his baggage and social inadequacies — wasn't bullied at Marjory Stoneman Douglas High School is being disingenuous.

| *"...hey this kid gets bullied a lot, please help him..."* |

After the massacre had taken place, eleventh grader, Maralo Alvarez, told reporters that he wished he'd spoken up for Cruz. "I could have said something to administrators, that 'hey this kid gets bullied a lot, please help him, please reach out to him.' I kind of regret not doing that," said the regretful student.[151]

Crus's own brother told the Palm Beach County Sheriff's Office that, "he and his friends, when they were younger, had bullied Nikolas, which he now regrets ever doing." Another instance was reported from a teenager from Washington state who chatted with Cruz on Instagram who said that Cruz was bullied a lot and "that he hated the school because of it."[152]

One of the many people who admittedly chose to bully Cruz rather than try to help him actually defended her bullying of the teenage boy with a straight face by stating, "Those talking about how we should not have ostracized him, you did not know this kid!" as if the fact that we personally didn't know that the kid was odd or different was justification for her to "ostracize" him. Please. Only a bully says something like that in defense of their actions. It's like the rapist saying, "Those talking about how we should not have raped that person, you did not know them."

Coincidentally, this same young woman — along with several other opportunistic children and adults — went on to take advantage of her newfound "popularity" by lazily attacking law-abiding gun owners' choices, rather than even attempting to shed any light on the negative affects bullying has on young people. I was personally appalled to see a national news media typically guided by feelings and virtue signaling, ditch their normal defense of bullied children and take this bullying young woman's side instead, simply because *they hated the Second Amendment more than they hated bullies.*

MEDICATED

Nikolas Cruz was no stranger to mood altering drugs. It's reported that doctors at Henderson Behavioral Health had prescribed him Focalin, Clonidine and Risperidone and during Cruz's confession he admitted to taking "lots of drugs," including Xanax and marijuana. The list of side effects he could expect to experience from the four prescription drugs alone (excluding the marijuana) include: hallucinations, behavior problems, aggression, hostility, paranoia, anxiety, depression, agitation, confusion, trouble thinking, impaired judgment, suicide, mania, feeling on edge, irritability, insomnia, nervousness, restlessness, abnormal dreams, fear, thoughts of hurting oneself, unusual risk taking, and no fear of danger. Really?! Are we really surprised this kid had issues?

To be clear, these drugs are meant to help people and I'm sure they do so daily. But a young person being on this many psychotropic drugs with this many negative side effects wreaks of an irresponsible treatment facility or, at best, an incompetent one.

WARNING SIGNS

Saying Nikolas Cruz "fell between the cracks" is like saying Fat Albert fell between the couch cushions. In fact, I've never seen so many serious warning signs that came up over and over again that officials either ignored or disregarded. I realize no one has a crystal ball to read into the future. I get that. And I don't support things like "red flag gun laws" when dealing with people and hypothetical crimes. But neighbors complained of harassment and threats by Cruz. There are documented reports of violent outbursts at home and at school by Cruz. He physically assaulted his own mother. He threatened people online. He commented at school and online about being the "next school shooter" and that he wanted to kill people. His mother said he was kicked out of school because he had said he was going to go there and blow all those people away.[153]

After Nikolas Cruz was reported as being the killer at Marjory Stoneman Douglas, no one who knew him was surprised. No one said, "He was such a nice guy" or "We never saw it coming" or "I can't believe he would do something like that." No one. In fact, most people who knew him felt that the killing spree was the logical next step in Cruz's life. Cruz was practically on everybody's radar in Parkland, FL.

Here are several of the documented incidents that told us we were dealing with a sociopath before Cruz's rampage killing at the school:[154]

- 19 documented statements of hatred towards groups or people

- 11 Statements of thoughts of killing or hurting people

- 8 knife/bullet/firearm seen in Cruz's possession

- 7 instances of animal cruelty

- 3 specific statements to shoot up school

| *"... they're letting a kid in the school that he's so violent and dangerous we won't let him in with his backpack..."*. |

State, local, and federal officials failed the people of Parkland, FL. Andrew Pollack's daughter, Meadow, was killed by Cruz and acknowledged the failures saying, "They didn't tell us that they're letting a kid in the school that he's so violent and dangerous we won't let him in with his backpack and we have to frisk him. But they let this kid into the school with our children."[155] Kelvin Greenleaf, who searched Cruz for weapons every morning before school stated, "I've seen kids who didn't act like Nikolas Cruz shoot up schools. So it's kind of — I don't try to, like, label my kids. I know he was different,"[156]

Stevie Wonder could've done a better job seeing the warning signs and acting on them than the authorities in Parkland, Florida did.

INCENTIVES FOR OFFICIALS TO LOOK THE OTHER WAY

The Broward County school district denied for months that Nikolas Cruz had any connection to an Obama-era incentive program created to reduce student arrests and even claimed that any story stating otherwise was "fake news". Then they gave in — or got tired of lying to people — and admitted that Cruz was in fact a part of their PROMISE (Preventing Recidivism Through Opportunities,

Mentoring, Interventions, Support & Education) program.[157]

The PROMISE Program was an alternative to arresting minority students involved in misdemeanors such as fighting, vandalism, theft and drug/alcohol use and required students to complete a program consisting of various forms of counseling for students, presumably circumventing the so-called "school to prison pipeline". Popular conservative analyst, Ben Shapiro, once stated that the PROMISE Program "had rewritten its disciplinary policies to make it nearly impossible to suspend, expel, or arrest students for behavioral problems including criminal activity."

| *...they were paid federal grant money through the program for every crime they essentially ignored...* |

The upside — for the school district and local law enforcement agencies — in participating in the PROMISE Program was that they were paid federal grant money through the program for every crime they essentially ignored. Everywhere monetary incentive programs have ever been created, corruption and deception have followed and the collateral damage is usually unnoticed and relatively harmless despite the wrongdoing. But in this case, 17 families still have many unanswered questions.

"This was the most avoidable school shooting in the history of the country." - Andrew Pollack.

111

Chapter 12: DEVIN KELLEY - SUTHERLAND SPRINGS

"Everybody dies, motherfuckers!" - *Devin Kelley right before killing 26 innocent churchgoers*

At roughly 11:20 a.m. in front of a convenience store in a quiet little town in South Texas, a suspicious man was reported across the street from the First Baptist Church there. He was dressed in all black tactical-style gear, wore a mask, and carried an AR-15. The man crept toward the church as a prayer service was underway inside. He opened fire as he approached the front entrance. He then promptly entered and continued firing indiscriminately.[158]

After allegedly firing nearly 700 rounds at innocent Americans as he stalked them from the center aisle of the First Baptist Church in Sutherland Springs, Texas, rampage killer, Devin Kelley, fled the scene after an AR-15-wielding Stephen Willeford confronted the demented killer, ending his rampage and thwarting further carnage. Inside the church lie 10 deceased women, 7 deceased men, 7 deceased girls, 1 deceased boy, and 1 deceased unborn child, along with 22 other innocent, wounded people who never knew their attacker.

Although I include Devin Kelley in this book, his past is the most difficult one to research because his rampage killing is so new, having taken place in 2017. In many cases, courts seal medical and other case records due to civil lawsuits by family members victims and in cases where fault may be assigned to anyone besides the killer. My point in saying all this is that while Kelley certainly fits with all of our other sociopaths, this chapter is a relatively short one based on limited available information.

BROKEN HOME

There's practically no information on Devin Kelley's early childhood. At the time of the killings, Kelley lived with his parent's in their $1 million home on a 28-acre piece of property with his parents.[159] That doesn't sound like too much of a broken home, but living in an expensive house isn't necessarily an indicator of a perfect home either.

BULLIED

Former classmates have described Devin Kelley as 'creepy', 'crazy' and an 'outcast'[160] Kelley's martial arts instructor said Kelley signed up for his class because he was being bullied and that he did not fit in. I could not confirm that information, but don't have any reason to doubt it based on all the other unusual and unacceptable things about Kelley. Other former classmates described him as a drifter, a loner, and — in some cases — a source of fear.[161] One former classmate had mentioned that Kelley "never really identified with a certain group" and never had a permanent group of friends.

At his court martial in 2012 for beating his wife and stepson, Kelley told the military officers sentencing him that his violent behavior was a result of the childhood bullying he had endured. He also mentioned that he had a religious awakening during his time in a holding cell.[162] Don't they all.

Often times young people are bullied due to awkward tendencies and poor social skills. This guy just sounds like a person no one wanted to be around because of his abrasive attitude. I'm not suggesting it's okay to bully a person like Kelley who appears to have been a complete jerk, but it's tough to expect other children to gravitate towards a person like Kelley. At some point, adults have got to be plugged in and aware enough of what's happening in children's daily lives for the sake of kids heading in a bad direction like Kelley and for the purpose of protecting other children.

MEDICATED

Kelley's autopsy report showed traces of benzodiazepines which are typically used for treating anxiety. While there are no reports of the specific benzodiazepine Kelley was taking, the most common benzodiazepines prescribed for anxiety today are Xanax (alprazolam), Klonopin (clonazepam), and Valium (diazepam) which can all worsen cases of pre-existing depression. Studies also suggest that they can lead to treatment-resistant depression. Worse yet, benzodiazepines can cause "emotional blunting or numbness and increase suicidal thoughts and feelings".[163] Kelley's symptoms are textbook examples of these side effects.

WARNING SIGNS

Devin Kelley was an absolute mess of a person. In high school, he was suspended 7 times for "falsifying records, insubordination, profanity and a drug-related offense."[164] In the Air Force, Kelley had been court martialed for repeatedly striking, kicking, and choking his then-wife, and then striking his stepson so hard that he broke the child's collarbone and caused bleeding on the brain. The Air Force described it as "a force likely to produce death or grievous bodily harm."[165] After being charged for this domestic abuse by the Air Force, Kelley made death threats against the superior officers who had brought the charges against him. He was also caught sneaking firearms onto Holloman Air Force Base[166] at one point and later making threats of self-harm to a coworker.[167]

In 2014, Kelley was cited for animal cruelty at an RV park after witnesses said he tackled his dog to the ground and proceeded to punch it repeatedly. According to the police report, witnesses said Kelley was "beating on the dog with both fists, punching it in the head and chest," and that "he could hear the suspect yelling at the dog and while he was striking it, the dog was yelping and whining. The suspect then picked up the dog by the neck into the air and threw it onto the ground and then drug him away to lot 60." What a guy.

ONCE AGAIN, PEOPLE ARE THE PROBLEM

If you were to listen to some politicians in Congress and all of the well-funded, anti-gun enterprises out there profiting off of hand-picked headlines, you'd swear that there were no background checks required to purchase guns from gun shops across America. You would believe that regardless of criminal history, anyone could waltz into any legitimate gun store and score a few handguns, a shotgun, and maybe an AR-15 without so much as a glancing look from the people running the business. This is a well-choreographed lie. It's quite likely that every single law-abiding gun owner in America already knows this. While this is purposeful propaganda by the anti-gun enterprises pushed onto many ignorant, group-thinking Americans, it's completely false and this anti-Constitutional movement knows it. The reason they keep repeating it is because idiots keep believing it.

However, the weakest link in nearly every process is almost always a person. The federal background check system relies on input from many different people in government agencies, including the military. In the case of how Devin Kelley managed to wrongly obtain firearms, the U.S. Air Force was that weak link. As referenced earlier, it failed to submit critical data and fingerprints that would've prevented Kelley from being able to legally purchase firearms. In fact, court filings stated that "inadequate training" led to the failure in reporting to the FBI. A colonel who was in charge of the region testified that it wasn't until after the shooting that he learned fingerprints and felony convictions must be reported to the FBI. This level of incompetence is coming from a colonel — in charge.[168]

Kelley had received a one-year sentence for threatening to kill his wife and for fracturing her son's skull. "Had his information been in the database, it should have prevented gun sales to Kelley," the Air Force said in a statement.[169]

The Air Force failed three other times to notify the FBI of events that should have triggered warnings and barred Kelley from legally obtaining weapons, according to the report.

- The first bungled chance occurred in June 2011 when Air Force authorities investigated Kelley for allegedly assaulting his stepchild. They collected Kelley's fingerprints but never submitted them to the FBI as required.

- The second lost opportunity happened in February 2012 after Kelley had been accused of beating his wife.

- The third time was in June 2012 when Air Force investigators didn't inform the FBI of Kelley's video confession that he had injured his stepson.

Kelley bought weapons four times when he should not have been able to because persons in the Air Force failed to submit appropriate data to the FBI to prevent the purchases, according to the inspector general's report.[170]

In a 2020 lawsuit by some of the victims' family members against the Untied States of America — namely the Air Force — under the heading "Negligent Undertaking", court papers stated the following:

"The Air Force's negligent undertaking looks like this: First, the Government issued regulations requiring the collection and submission of fingerprints and final dispositions of felons and domestic violence perpetrators to the FBI. Second, it issued supporting regulations—such as requiring documentation and retention of case files—to catch failures to submit criminal history. And third, after investigations by the Inspector General, it agreed to correct its fail- ures to collect and submit criminal history. Each of these efforts should have ensured that Devin Kelley's fingerprints and criminal history were in the FBI's background check system.5 But the Government failed to exercise reasonable care in performing its obligations, which prevented that result. This increased the risk of harm to the public and resulted in actual physical harm."[171]

This was no small oversight. Innocent people were murdered in cold blood as a result of clerical errors and training dereliction. Kelley's deadly missed opportunity is only one of more than 7,000 U.S. Air Force airmen between 1998 and 2017 whose criminal histories were not properly reported to the FBI database.[172]

CHAPTER 13: DISHONORABLE MENTION

"I made 'Bowling for Columbine' in the hope the school shootings would stop and that we would address the issue of how easy it is to get a gun in the United States, and tragically, those school shootings continue. — **Michael Moore** *(Someone please tell Moore that the reason "school shootings" didn't stop is because he was wrong about the cause of them.)*

In my efforts to write this book, I was met with overwhelming evidence that rampage killers were mostly from broken homes, were bullied, and they were medicated. I say *mostly* because in some cases I can't be sure that *all* rampage killers possessed all 3 of these causal factors and I don't want to be the least bit deceptive in the information I put out because this topic is so important to me. Some of the sociopaths in this book had been bullied and medicated, but appeared to be from a perfectly good home. Sadly, history is littered with children who were abused by family members, but there had been little to no signs of it. And some rampage killers didn't have clear evidence that they were medicated. In some cases this is due to cases still being tied up in litigation along with medical records that are sealed. In one specific instance, the killer had been medicated, but his medical records were sealed so as not to create a stigma for the pharmaceutical company. You read that correctly.

119

Sadly, there are countless rampage killers to research. Outside of the ones I highlighted in previous chapters, I wanted to include some of the other killers who were a little more recognizable, but may have either had limited data to discuss in detail on them or they didn't clearly have all of the "devil's triangle" causal factors outlined in the book. Here are some of those:

JAMES HOLMES

This coward — like most killers do — purposely chose this gun-free movie theater in Aurora, Colorado knowing that none of the 420 innocent people he'd be shooting at inside would be armed and provide any level of resistance. After all the smoke had settled following James Holmes' attack, 12 innocent people had been murdered and another 70 more were wounded.

- BROKEN HOME: Holmes' father worked as a mathematician and scientist while his mother was a registered nurse. While there aren't any reports of his home life being a negative force in his life, there are reports that when he was 11 he'd attempted suicide.

- BULLIED: Holmes is one of the subjects I felt like needed to be in this book because evidence shows that he was very much affected by his prescribed medications. But I could find no data that indicated he was bullied. One report claimed that "Holmes was the first kid picked by his peers to be on sports teams because everyone knew he was a fast runner".[173] While Holmes certainly wasn't the life of the party as he was not overly social and was an odd person, it doesn't appear that bullying was a big causal factor for him.

- MEDICATED: Psychiatrist Lynne Fenton prescribed Holmes the drug, Zoloft, which is used to treat depression, panic disorder and obsessive-compulsive disorder along with the drug, Klonopin, prescribed to treat anxiety and panic attacks. When being interviewed after the killings, court-appointed psychiatrist Dr. William Reid commented to Holmes, "It sounds a little like you're saying, if you hadn't had the medication, the shootings never would have taken place." Holmes replied, "I'd say it was a possibility."[174]

OMAR MATEEN

This killer is a tough one to nail down. Mateen killed 49 people and wounded 53 in the second deadliest rampage killing in modern U.S. history. Mateen was a professed "Islamic soldier" and pledged allegiance to the Islamic State militant group.[175] I tried hard not to include scumbag's who were specifically committed racists or religious nut bags who killed for those reasons because their causal factors had a bit of a twist driven by unhinged personal beliefs. On top of his idiotic religious beliefs, it appeared that he was a closet homosexual[176] and was ashamed of that. Some suggest this is why his assault was at a gay nightclub where he was a regular. One Pulse nightclub regular even commented, "I think it's possible that he was trying to deal with his inner demons, of trying to get rid of his anger of homosexuality. It's really confusing to me. Because you can't change who you are. But if you pretend that you're different, then you may shoot up a gay bar."[177]

If Mateen was, in fact radicalized, and a gay man, it's likely he was tormented with internal conflicts of being a gay muslim as "Islamic law as derived from scripture not only condemns, but prescribes cruel and unusual punishments for homosexuality".[178]

- BROKEN HOME: The only evidence I could find of Mateen having a broken home was that his father was openly homophobic and in complete denial of Mateen's homosexual double life. He even commented after Mateen's rampage killing that he was saddened by his son's actions during the Muslim holy month of Ramadan, but made sure to add "God will punish those involved in homosexuality" and adding that it's "not an issue that humans should deal with."[179] This kind of strict, orthodox Islamic ideology surely made it impossible for Mateen to "come out" or express himself, let alone talk about being gay with his family.

- BULLIED: NPR reported that Mateen "was bullied as a kid in school. He had well-documented behavioral problems. He was aggressive toward other kids".[180] This was the only report of Mateen being bullied as a child. But let's remember that 64% of students who are bullied do not report it.[181]

- MEDICATED: Mateen's ex-wife said he had a history of steroid use[182] and a medical examiner later found evidence of physical changes to Mateen's body that were consistent with long-term steroid use in his autopsy report.[183] Much of the data on the long-term effects of steroids comes from case reports rather than epidemiological studies and show that some of the serious side effects of long-term prednisone use are depression and psychotic behavior.[184] Steroids may not be "psychiatric" drugs, but evidence shows that it can certainly alter a person's personality in a very negative way.

STEPHEN PADDOCK

After gambling far into the early morning hours of September 27 in the casino, Stephen Paddock spoke with the Mandalay Bay VIP host referencing the "Vista Suite" in the 200 Wing of the casino hotel. Paddock was polite, but firm on his insistence on booking the suite. He was considered a "high roller" based on the amount of money he routinely spent at areas casinos which gave him a higher than average level of influence. Paddock stressed that the suite had a "better view".[185]

On October 1, 2017, Paddock executed the worst rampage killing in U.S. history, killing 59 innocent people and wounding another 500 at a concert in Las Vegas.

- BROKEN HOME: When Stephen Paddock was just 7 years old, he became fatherless in the most untraditional way — his father was captured in Las Vegas for bank robbery and imprisoned later in 1961. Benjamin Paddock escaped from prison in 1969 and spent an impressive 9 years on the lamb until he was recaptured in Oregon in 1978.[186] He had been wanted for numerous bank robberies and even spent time on the FBI's Most Wanted list.[187]

- BULLIED: I could find no evidence that Paddock was bullied growing up. But with him being so much older than most other rampage killers, data on him as a child and young man just isn't out there.

- MEDICATED: Paddock once bragged that he had a unique relationship with a doctor who prescribed him Valium when he wanted it saying of the doctor, "He's like on retainer, I call it, I guess. It means I pay a fee yearly...I have good access to him." Traces of Valium (diazepam) were found in Paddock's urine instead of his bloodstream which shows that the Valium may have been mostly out of his system and not affected his behavior. Diazepam is a sedative-hypnotic drug in the class of drugs known as benzodiazepines — for anxiousness and withdrawal effects are rage and aggressiveness and can last for weeks and even years. In a 2015 study of 960 adults and teens convicted of homicide showed that their odds of killing were 45 percent higher during time periods when they were on benzodiazepines like diazepam.[188]

STEVEN KAZMIERCZAK

Steven Kazmierczak checked in to Room 105 at the DeKalb Travelodge by simply signing his name as "Steven". Over the course of the next couple of days, he smoked several packs of cigarettes, took a few doses of over the counter cold medicine, and knocked back a number of cans of Red Bull energy drink. Also with him were three handguns, a pump shotgun, and a duffle bag full of ammunition.

Six shotgun rounds and 47 pistol rounds later on the afternoon of February 14, 2008, Kazmierczak lay motionless on his back in the Cole Hall Auditorium Room 101 in a shirt that read "TERRORIST" on it with a pool of blood draining out of the back of his head. After killing 5 students and injuring 17 more, Kazmierczak had shot himself in the head.

- BROKEN HOME: There's a good bit of information on Kazmierczak, but the only information pointing to any major disruptions at home were his sister's claims that "he was verbally abusive and aggressive toward his mother and her and that he was the cause of significant disruption within the family".[189] However, after reports detailing the inside of the Travelodge Kazmierczak stayed in preparing for his rampage killing being littered with cigarette butts, his father, Robert Kazmierczak, suspected that someone else may have been involved because he said Steven didn't smoke. No one else was involved. Steven Kazmierczak did smoke. According to autopsy reports, nicotine was found in his system.[190] His father apparently didn't know his son like he thought he did.

- BULLIED: "For as long as I can remember, I have always been an extremely sensitive individual and feel as though I am able to empathize with other people's emotional and social needs," Kazmierczak had previously written. "However, some of my peers were not very understanding or accepting, and I feel as though I was victimized to a certain degree during my adolescent years."[191] There's not a lot of supporting information out there on Kamierczak being bullied other than this quote and an Esquire story that stated that he allegedly was bullied in high school. His unusual personality and poor social skills, however, likely made him a target of bullies throughout his school years.

- MEDICATED: Kazmierczak had been prescribed and took Prozac, Xanax, and Ambien. He allegedly had stopped taking his Prozac about three weeks before his killings "because it made him feel like a zombie," his girlfriend reported.[192] Prozac has serious withdrawal side effects and is also slower to leave a patient's body once they stop taking it due to it's longer "half life" — the length of time it takes for 50% of a medication to leave the body once it's discontinued. According to Medical News Today, "doctors do not recommend stopping antidepressant use abruptly because it may lead to more severe symptoms."[193]

CHAPTER 14: OTHER COMMONALITIES

"Dear Principal, In a few hours you will probably hear about a school shooting in North Carolina. I am responsible for it." — *Alvaro Castillo, obsessed with Eric Harris, sent this email to Columbine High School the morning he killed his father and two students at his school in North Carolina[194]*

While so many of these rampage killers I researched are from broken homes, have been bullied, and are on psychotropic drugs, not all of them fall into these three categories. The extensive event correlation performed in this book and the 3 main causal factors it produced is not meant to force a particular point or certainly not to mistakenly eliminate focus on any other similarities between rampage killers. All of these commonalities are critical to us being able to recognize warning signs that may be able to tip us off when a person needs help.

OFTEN A LIFE CRISIS TRIGGERS THEIR RAMPAGE

Many rampage killers have a triggering event that set them off — sort of a "last straw". Violence very rarely blows up without signs of escalation. Behavioral cues are typically a hint at impending danger from an individual.[195] Here are some noticeable "triggering" events.

Adam Lanza: Lanza and his mother were the only ones living in their relatively large home. This home was one that had become somewhat of a "comfortable prison" for Lanza as he was overly sensitive to any kind of change. Mrs. Lanza was planning to downsize and this required her and her son to sell they home and move to a new house in a new area. This was a major unsettling change that Adam Lanza was not prepared to deal with. It's possible this pending life-changing event was too much for Lanza to contemplate prior to making his decision to attack Sandy Hook Elementary School in Newtown, CT.

Nikolas Cruz: Cruz was admittedly a "momma's boy". His mother pampered him endlessly and may have even enabled Cruz's bad behavior to a certain degree. Mrs. Cruz passed away suddenly and Cruz and his brother had to find a place to live. Nikolas Cruz moved in with a friend and the friend's parents. Cruz initiated his massacre at Marjory Stoneman Douglas High School in Parkland, FL just three months later.

Recognizing these life crisis triggers doesn't always help us in terms of identifying a potential killer ahead of time since once that trigger does occur they usually execute whatever plan they have very shortly thereafter. But I do think that if there's an individual that's being watched because he has the three main factors we've discussed in the book or any

129

others we've discussed here, it may behoove us to keep a closer eye on them in the event of a breakup, bullying episode, death of a close family member, etc. to maybe catch an escalation before it can evolve into a rampage killing.

THEY STUDY AND IDOLIZE PAST RAMPAGE KILLERS

Many rampage killers become transfixed with past rampage killers. They research minute details of their past and of their killings. Psychologist Dr. Peter Langham has done extensive research into the unusual interconnections among these types of killers and stated that these individuals see themselves as "joining a subculture in which they are not only normal, but perhaps feel themselves to be special, apart from and above mainstream society."[196]

Probably the most researched rampage killer is Columbine mastermind, Eric Harris. With the Columbine killing being one of the first in this era of the 24 hours news cycle, it seems to have become sort of a twisted measuring stick for these individuals.

Sueng-Hui Cho: Immediately after the Columbine murders, a classmate of the Virginia Tech killer once stated how much 15-year-old Cho had become obsessed with Eric Harris and Dylan Klebold stating, "I remember sitting in Spanish class with him, right next to him, and there being something written on his binder to the effect of, you know, '

'F' you all, I hope you all burn in hell,' which I would assume meant us, the students."[197]

Alex Hribal: Hribal's 2014 knife attack on a Pennsylvania school was preceded by him writing, "I became a prophet because I spread the word of god, Eric Harris."[198]

Randy Stair: This Pennsylvania rampage killer later wrote, "I love you, Eric Harris, you da man."[199]

While this may not be a causal factor like the main ones in this book, researching past rampage killers is definitely an easy-to-spot commonality that family members, teachers, and fellow students could pick up on early. Their research could be a matter of these individuals reading other killers' manifestos and suicide letters or just searching them out on the internet. Either way, unless you're writing a book on it, taking a deep dive into the lives of rampage killers to the point of obsessing over it is certainly a warning sign of possible things to come.

THEY HAVE ABUSED, THREATENED, OR WRITTEN ABOUT IT BEFORE

Before rampage killers kill, they usually assault, abuse or threaten people and sometimes animals they have access to and in many cases they write about it on social media or in other forms of writings. These are all very clear signals for us to keep an eye out for in terms of recognizing cries for help.

Sueng-Hui Cho: Lucinda Roy, head of the Virginia Tech English Department during Cho's junior year, said he began writing things in class that were filled with anger and violent fantasies. "I thought he was maybe suicidal, he just seemed so depressed and I was also just concerned with him in general..."[200]

Nikolas Cruz: Before killing 17 people at a school in Parkland, Florida, Cruz is said to have talked about shooting small animals, including lizards, squirrels, frogs, and a neighbor's chickens, and reportedly sent his dog to a neighbor's house to attack the pigs there.[201] Mrs. Cruz's friend, Marni Garvey of Coral Springs, said Cruz had "screaming episodes" and would tell his mother to "go fuck herself" and "I wish you to die" and that "he pushed her, you know, he was very violent with her."[202]

Devin Kelley: Kelley was cited for animal cruelty in El Paso County on August 1, 2014, (3 years before his rampage) after numerous witnesses saw him at an RV park on the ground beating his dog in the head and neck area.[203] Ironically, Kelley's LinkedIn page listed "animal welfare" as one of the causes he cared about.[204]

Adam Lanza: Before his Sandy Hook rampage killing in 2012, Lanza wrote online in 2011 that "— serial killers are lame. Everyone knows that mass murderers are the cool kids."[205]

THEY CHOOSE GUN-FREE ZONES

Economist John R. Lott correctly identifies gun-free zones as "places where only police or military policy are classified, places where it is illegal to carry a permitted concealed handgun, places that are posted as not allowing a permitted concealed handgun, places where 'general citizens' are not allowed to obtain permits or where permits are either not issued to any general citizens or to only a very tiny selective segment."[206] Lott's claim that 98% of "mass shootings" take place in gun-free zones[207] is disputed by the anti-gun group Everytown For Gun Safety who laughingly claim that only 10% of "mass shootings" take place in gun-free zones. This is an extraordinary lie, but it's based on their own shady definition of gun-free zones that reads "areas where civilians are prohibited from carrying firearms and there is not a regular armed law enforcement presence." Confusing? Well, let me help put that one into context by pointing out that Everytown doesn't count the Ft. Hood rampage shooting as being in a gun-free zone even though civilians and non-military police personnel are prohibited from carrying firearms on base. Sounds pretty clear to me!

It's an indisputable fact that killers of all kinds choose gun-free zones because of lack of resistance associated with good guys with guns. According to the United States Concealed Carry Association (USCCA), below is a list of federally designated areas where weapons are banned, even with a permit:

- Federal Courthouses*
- Federal Buildings*
- Any Building Owned, Leased or Rented by the Federal Government — This includes buildings in national forests which are property of the federal government.
- National Forests — There is no federal law prohibiting carry in national forests. States control the carrying of firearms in national forests in their state. However, carry is not allowed buildings in national forests which are property of the federal government.
- Visitors Centers/Ranger Stations in National Parks — These are federal buildings where carry is not allowed. There is no federal law that prohibits carry in national parks. States control the carrying of firearms in national parks in their state.
- Sterile areas of Airports -An individual may not have a weapon on or about the individual's person or accessible property when entering or in a sterile area of an airport or when attempting to board or onboard an aircraft for which screening is conducted.
- Federal Prisons*
- U.S. Army Corps of Engineers* — The Corps builds and runs flood control and navigation dams. The Corps has jurisdiction over the dam site and usually all waters backed up by the dam. Per 36 CFR § 327.13, carry anywhere on Corps property is illegal unless written permission has been received from the District Commander. Firearms can be

unloaded and secured in a vehicle while on Corps property.

- National Cemeteries*
- Military Bases — All military bases are Federal property. Each base may have slightly different policies, however visitors who arrive at a military base with firearm(s) must leave them with the guards at the gate. If the base does not have storage capabilities at the gate or armory, you could be turned away. The only people who can carry guns around a base—concealed or otherwise—are on-duty military police, who handle routine security. They then have to return their guns to the armory when their shifts are over. There are exceptions for on-duty local or state police officers who come to the base on official business. The base commander can make other exceptions. Check at each military post for specific rules. Exception-Active duty military police, criminal investigators, and Marine Corps law enforcement program police officers may conceal carry personally owned weapons while on base while off-duty as long as they comply with the 2016 Department of Defense Directive, title "Arming and the Use of Force".
- Rented Offices — Any part of any building that the federal government has rented for office space or a federal workforce, etc. Just their offices or the part of the building the federal government has control over is off-limits. You can carry in the rest of the building *if* state or local laws allow.
- Post Office — Postal regulations prohibit the possession of firearms in their buildings *and* in their parking lots or any property they own.

- Bureau of Land Management (BLM)* — On most BLM lands, if you can legally carry in the state the BLM land is in, you can carry on the BLM land. If it is not legal, the area will be posted as no firearms allowed. Any building on the BLM land operated by the federal government is considered federal property and carry in those buildings is not allowed. The exceptions where the BLM prohibits firearms are the San Pedro Riparian Zone in Arizona, the Wallace Conservation Forest in Idaho and Red Rock National Conservation Area in Nevada.

- Indian Reservations — Carry on Indian Reservations is controlled by tribal law. You must check with each tribe before carrying on the property. Some Indian tribes consider federal and state highways through their property as under their control. This should also be verified with the tribe.

* This includes parking lots adjacent to, or part of, the facility if the federal entity owns or has control of the parking lot and it is posted "No Firearms." The lot has to be posted under federal law (below) if they do not wish to have firearms present.[208]

Keep your head on a swivel in these places!

In today's day of immediate access to pretty much any information, it's important to present data as truthfully as possible since you can be outed pretty easily for fudging numbers to fit your political agenda. We can argue about whether or not most rampage killings take place in gun-free zones all day, based on whatever definition you choose to use to support the position you hold. But as long as innocent people — and more importantly children — are left unprotected in these environments that rampage killers purposely continue to choose for whatever their reasons are, we are as complicate as the killers themselves if we put more effort into arguing what the definition of "gun-free zone" is as opposed to working to develop a way to secure their safety.

Our children are sitting ducks in these soft targets we call schools. My son deserves better. Your children deserve better.

CHAPTER 15: WHAT WE CAN DO

Dr. Joseph Glenmullen, Harvard Professor of Psychiatry, emphasizing that the psychiatric symptoms of antidepressant withdrawal are not a return of the patient's mental condition "...rather they are drug-induced withdrawal phenomena."

As stated earlier, if you make the conscious decision not to legitimately seek out the true root cause of any problem, then you aren't serious about solving that problem and shouldn't complain about it. Now, I don't expect everyone out there to *want* to seek out the true root cause of why killers kill. But if you aren't serious about trying to find out why rampage killers make the decision to indiscriminately murder other innocent people, yet you run out and sob and whine about how badly you wish the problem would end whenever one of these events takes place and then you proclaim that you won't stop fighting until these killings stop, then you should shut up. Just shut up. You are a liar and a fraud. You're actually worse than a run-of-the-mill liar, you're evil. Only an evil person could chase a camera down after a rampage killing, fake being sad and concerned, hug victims and victims' families, yet do nothing to pursue and prevent the problem from happening again. In my mind, you are only slightly better than rapists and child molesters.

By exclaiming, "When are we going to have the courage to put an end to these senseless acts of 'gun violence'" every time someone decides to murder someone else with a gun, these fake hacks pretend to take a moral high ground as if they're the experts, they've done the work, and they're just waiting on the rest of America to get on board with their bright idea of banning and limiting guns. Let me be clear — *they're no experts, they've done no work, and they don't have a single idea that would 1) prevent a single person from making the decision to kill someone else, and 2) not infringe upon the Second Amendment.* But it is possible to care about the Second Amendment *and* want to truly end rampage killings while protecting our children.

BE A BETTER PARENT, FRIEND, NEIGHBOR, AND TEACHER

I don't care who you talk to or what they tell you, no one had a perfect childhood growing up. Everyone has dealt with challenges at home and at school with varying degrees of severity. In most cases of rampage killers, any number of people could and should have recognized the signs of stressors affecting their behavior. The outward symptoms of trouble aren't hard to spot.

As parents, friends, neighbors, and teachers, there are many things that we likely witness and then dismiss or don't take note of.

- **Changes in behavior:** If a child is bubbly and cheerful and suddenly becomes depressed or sad, observe them from a distance to see if you can tell what's affecting them. Many children won't open up right away, but pull them aside in complete privacy and just talk to them about what might be bothering them. It could be home life, bad grades, being bullied, etc. Pay particular attention to episodes of aggression towards people or animals which can be a very solid early sign of major changes in behavior.

- **Trust your instincts:** Many times the things you suspect as being not quite right are exactly what you thought they were. Trust your senses and observe and intervene. I think we'd all be surprised how good it would make some kids feel knowing that someone seemed like they cared about them.

- **Oversee tech interaction:** Texting and social media are probably the quickest ways to know something is not going according to plan in a child's life. But being aware of their online search history is huge. Many of the rampage killers I researched not only heavily researched past rampage killers, but some searched for how to obtain weapons and even how to make bombs. That's a far cry for hunting down cheat codes for the latest video game.

- **Don't be afraid to intervene:** Puberty can release a sea of hormones that greatly affects young people's moods and personalities. Something as simple as them feeling as though their privacy isn't being respected can set them off. But we can be respectful of our kids' privacy and still be acutely aware of what's happening in their lives. And we owe it to them to do just that. If we get to a point where something just isn't right, it's unlikely that it'll just work itself out without possibly getting worse first. One instance of early intervention could be the difference in a child making a bad decision that affects them for the rest of their life.

- **Work to gain our kids' trust:** If our kids don't trust us, they won't listen to us. As parents, friends, neighbors, and teachers, if we can connect with kids then we're in their circle and we're much more likely to get helpful information out of them. As adults, we have lots going on in our lives, but so do our kids. We can't expect our kids to stand by and wait for our lives to slow down before they live theirs. We're the adults. We should be the ones more capable of dealing with adversity than them. We should always be willing to pump the breaks on the basic challenges of our adult lives in order to address the issues in our children's.

FIND OUT HOW A CHILD LEARNS AND TEACH THEM THAT WAY

My son used to go to an ABA (applied behavioral analysis) therapy center that had a sign above its door that read "If your child doesn't learn the way we teach, we'll teach the way they learn". What an awesome message! At least it sounded good when read from a sign on a wall. But if you don't back it up with your actions and teaching methods, it's just a sign on a wall. The therapy center had an unqualified guy who would copy things out of a text book and try to force my son to learn the way his text book told him to teach. This is an absolute guaranteed way to fail in the autism world. You can't force these kids to learn your way just because you're lazy or unqualified. The same concept applies to every other kid out there today.

The number of challenges facing young people today is overwhelming. Family units are splintered, the education system is a wreck, kids can be bullied online and not even know it until they show up for school the next day, and various political parties fight to maintain control over the systemic indoctrination of kids from pre-K through college to think and act the way they want them to.

| *We need to return to the days of letting children be unique without trying to force them into a box.* |

The biggest disappointments to me are the likes of the ridiculous programs like No Child Left Behind and its replacement, Every Student Succeeds, along with the shortage of teachers who actually care about the children themselves. We need to return to the days of letting children be unique without trying to force them into a box. Teachers should stop being *inconvenienced* by children who find it difficult to learn. If a child can succeed learning a different way, then get out of their way and let them learn. It's not supposed to be about you! I don't mean there shouldn't be boundaries or that every one of the millions of kids out there should have a custom lesson plan. But find out what interests a kid. If a kid has to read a page in a chemistry text book five times and still can't retain anything on it, it doesn't mean they're stupid or need to be medicated. It may just mean that they aren't the least bit interested in chemistry. Instead of pushing them onto some ADHD drug that drives them into a depression, maybe find out what interests them. Maybe they can dismantle a gas combustion engine in an hour and put it back together in their sleep. The world needs mechanics just as badly as we need chemists. Not all kids are meant for college and that's fine! They should be told that that's fine without belittling them.

| *Statistics in the early 2000's show a sharp uptick in the number of children who were medicated and ones with ADHD at about the same time No Child Left Behind was implemented.* |

Parents should also do all we can to help push to eliminate the use of standardized testing and "teaching to the test" programs like "No Child Left Behind" and the newer "Every Student Succeeds." These kinds of accountability laws where schools and teachers are rewarded or punished based on the scores school children make are not only encouraging a one-size-fits all approach to teaching, but it also creates a scenario where teachers and administrators enter a type of survival mode in order to provide for their own families' well being. This can push them to encourage parents to unnecessarily medicate overly active children in order to make the children more "teachable." Statistics in the early 2000's show a sharp uptick in the number of children who were medicated and ones with ADHD at about the same time No Child Left Behind was implemented. This is no coincidence.

HELP OUR KIDS OVERCOME BULLYING

The Centers for Disease Control and Prevention (CDC) defines bullying as "any unwanted aggressive behavior(s) by another youth or group of youths, who are not siblings or current dating partners, that involves an observed or perceived power imbalance, and is repeated multiple times or is highly likely to be repeated."[209] Almost, but not quite. This definition seems to be consistent with the CDC's recent lack of consistency. Clearly siblings, family members, and dating partners can all bully just like any other bully can. One's social or familial status does not determine whether or not what is happening to them may or may not be defined as bullying. But the CDC has proven — at least during the course of their constantly changing coronavirus escapades — that they are not the best equipped at dealing with many issues in spite of all the money they're paid. So, I'll give them a pass.

However, the American Psychological Association defines bullying as "a form of aggressive behavior in which someone intentionally and repeatedly causes another person injury or discomfort. Bullying can take the form of physical contact, words, or more subtle actions."[210] Boom! Short, sweet, and clear.

Bullying can have negative effects on everyone when it takes place — from the bully, the bullied, and even the witnesses who either see hope in it being dealt with properly or the lack of hope when it's not.

- YES, VIOLENCE IS PART OF THE ANSWER

We often hear the phrase "violence isn't the answer" or something related to that. Well, when it comes to bullying, violence can absolutely be the answer. When an entire school — including teachers and administrators — watch a child get bullied by peers and no one says or does anything to help, a well-placed punch can be the most glorious answer to whatever the question may have been. Just because other kids or teachers may not think the bullying of a particular child is severe and that it's not really a big deal, doesn't mean it's not. To that kid being bullied, it is a *very* big deal. Imagine the sense of hopelessness knowing that you can't defend yourself because you'll be expelled and that no one else — including teachers and staff — have any intention of helping you. Talk about being on a deserted island all by yourself!

- WHAT IF WE APPLIED "ZERO TOLERANCE" TO ADULTS

I would personally like to meet the idiots who thought it was a good idea to implement a policy that punishes a child who is attacked by a bully and that the bullied child should receive the same punishment as his attacker. Read that again if you need to. What an absolutely moronic, nonsensical thing to suggest. Did actual bullies come up with this?

To fully appreciate how ridiculous "zero tolerance" — or punishing victims the same as we do offenders — is, let's look at some adult scenarios with ZT employed:

- I'm cutting my grass in my yard one sunny Saturday. I cross the front of my yard to head down the side of my yard where it meets my neighbor's property. My neighbor is standing there with a friend, watching me. As I drive by he pushes me off my lawnmower for no reason and they both start laughing. I get off the ground and walk up to him — on my property — and ask him what the problem is. He starts shoving me and telling me to F off. What do I do? I'm in immediate danger. This is an unprovoked situation. But I'm afraid of our city's new "zero tolerance" law. The guy keeps shoving me, so I shove him back and into his yard where he falls down. The police are driving by at that very moment and saw the whole thing. They quickly shove both of us to the ground and cuff us. "Minimum of 20 years in prison for both of you," one officer says. "What?!" I exclaim. "You guys watched the whole thing! How am I in trouble for defending myself?" One officer turns to me as he shoves me into the back of his patrol car and says, "Zero tolerance, sir."

- I'm sipping a cold drink in my backyard, about to hop in the pool to cool off when out of nowhere this big bag of garbage comes flying over the fence and lands in my pool. Yep, it's that a-hole neighbor again. I quickly jump into the pool, grab the bag of trash, and throw it back over the fence into his yard. The neighbor calls the cops on me. The cops show up to my house to question me, but I have an ace up my sleeve — my security cameras caught the whole thing. I show the law enforcement officers the video and they promptly slap cuffs on me. "20 years, sir," he states. "Ever heard of zero tolerance? You people need to learn that we are the only ones who can defend you."

- I'm sitting on my front porch enjoying the weather. Suddenly my neighbor runs into my yard and throws something at me that hits me in my chest. He looks back at his buddy in his yard and starts to laugh as I realize he's just thrown dog feces on me. I pick up the K-9 dung and heave it back at him, hitting him in the face. My wife calls the police. Fortunately for me, the neighbor across the street saw the whole thing and will tell the police. But that doesn't matter — because zero tolerance. My neighbor is hauled off to jail and I'm in the patrol car right behind him.

Why does zero tolerance seem so stupid when we apply it to adults, but it's perfectly okay applied to children?

| *Why are we ok with punishing innocent children who are fed up with being attacked?* |

Why are we ok with punishing innocent children who are fed up with being attacked? How do we sleep at night knowing we've created a defective system where kids walk on egg shells through 12 years of government schooling? I hope every single teacher and administrator who pushed for zero tolerance and who's ever looked the other way when witnessing bullying has sleepless nights for the rest of their miserable lives. I'm sorry, but I'm not that overly noble person who just wants to turn the other cheek and sing and dance together. If an innocent person cries out for help and they don't get it, I'm ok with some eye-for-an-eye style justice going down. If you aren't okay with that then implement better policy!

- IS VIOLENCE THE ONLY ANSWER?

If innocent children were able to defend themselves from bullies without receiving the same punishment as their attackers, this book would be a lot shorter. But we still have imbeciles in charge of our government education policies, so this is what we're dealing with. Think of all the other countries in the world kicking the United States' butts in education. How many of those do you think teach elementary school kids how to masturbate? How many do you think teach kids that certain people of a certain skin color are automatically evil just because of their skin color?

How many of those do you think would sentence an innocent child — who finally gets up enough courage to defend himself — to the same sentence as the hateful kid who's been repeatedly terrorizing them?

Are there other "answers" besides allowing a kid to fight back? Of course there are:

- Completely do away with "zero tolerance" policies and allow a system to be implemented similar to a real world system that looks at each individual instance of violence or disruption on its own. If Billy punches John in the mouth because there was a proven history of Billy being physically pushed around or beaten up by John, then Billy should be spoken to about other potential ways to de-escalate situations without violence whenever possible, but not punished. He should have to fill out an incident report documenting why he defended himself and what happened. John, on the other hand, should be suspended and a record kept of the entire incident. Future instances would result in escalating consequences. In the real world, we call bullying by different, more serious sounding terms — harassment and assault. If my neighbor "bullies" me, he could go to jail. But they don't send me to jail for defending myself from him. Why do we do that to kids in school? Are we really that lazy and aloof when it comes to our children?

- Teachers could pull the bullies aside and talk to them one-on-one — seriously. Naturally a bully will be defiant and maybe even make it worse on his target if he's approached or questioned in front of those he so desperately feels the need to impress. But if he's pulled aside and spoken to away from his audience about consequences of his actions and about how he'd feel if he were bullied himself, we might get somewhere. But it takes that teacher not taking the easy way out. It takes a little compassion. We hear all the time that teachers enter their profession because they love children and want to devote their lives to teaching them, but then so many look the other way when witnessing bullying because addressing it isn't worth their time or important to them. Where's that love of the children we all sang around the campfire about? Is that only when the popular kid makes straight A's?

- The bully and the child reporting it should be counseled separately and in private. First, the bullied needs to be comfortable reporting details and should not feel ashamed or intimidated by other people overhearing the conversation. Second, reports show that many bullies have psychosocial issues of their own and in many cases are even bullied themselves. The conversation with them could be therapeutic for them and even end up solving more issues than just the one at hand.

- Shame bullying. That's right, I said it. Many times, all a bully wants is to be seen as the "cool kid." If they and all other kids in school are conditioned to see bullying as what failures do and "not cool", they are less likely to want to be "that guy." I make no apologies for this. Bullying should be put in the same category as being a criminal and spoken about with the same disdain and disgust. You rarely see kids ashamed of being a bully or proud to be a criminal. In this case, though, be careful not to shame the child who's doing the bullying in case they're dealing with the issues I point out in the previous bullet point. The act of bullying should be shamed, not the child.

- Parents have to create an environment where our children feel comfortable and unashamed coming to us with problems they encounter at school, including being bullied. No instance being reported should ever be minimized where a child feels like he or she is being blown off.

- Install video surveillance cameras in every square inch of a school except for restrooms and locker rooms. This is cheap to do with today's available technology. I have over a dozen high definition, color cameras all around my home that record audio and video. I did this all for a little over $1,000.00. Don't tell me we can't do that in schools. We all know why many teachers and administrators don't want video cameras throughout schools and in classes. Accountability in ones job can be a little intimidating when you're not a good employee.

- Never take a single report of bullying lightly — ever! When a child musters up enough courage to actually report bullying, it should always be treated as if escalation could result in a possible rampage killing. I'm certainly not suggesting that it will. I'm simply pointing out that there should always be a sense of urgency when a case is reported. Downplaying the occurrence takes the wind out of the bullied kid's sails and conditions he or she to feel that reporting bullying is useless because nothing will be done about it. The bully should always feel as if the teacher or administrator is slightly overreacting to the occurrence. That's proof that it's being dealt with properly and with authority. If we're going to develop a system to manage and eliminate bullying, the process has to be rock solid and fully administered in every case.

- Leadership in schools is where it all starts. If leadership feels that bullying is just something that happens and can't be prevented, that school can't even begin to solve the problem of bullying. If leadership doesn't understand that bullying can produce lifelong negative consequences and that it should be rooted out and dealt with firmly, then you have the wrong leader. These leaders can be as high up as superintendents and principals or as frontline as counselors and teachers.

I'm going to say this and I have no way of proving it, but I'm going to say it as loudly as I can anyway and for anyone who will listen:

"If there were no bullied children, there would be far fewer rampage killers."

Prove me wrong.

DEVELOP ANONYMOUS REPORTING METHODS

There are a few programs out there that allow people to anonymously report child abuse and neglect as well as potential dangers from dangerous people. With the threat of potential blowback and retaliation by some children and even parents these days, I can see why so many instances go unreported and why many people wouldn't want to "get involved." But that cannot be our reason for not sitting it out when we could be helping so many of our kids who need help.

Inspired by the unspeakable rampage killing that occurred at Columbine High School in 1999, the state of Colorado created an amazing program called *Safe 2 Tell Colorado.* They found that "in 81% of violent incidents in U.S. schools, someone other than the attacker knew it was going to happen but failed to report it."[211] According to their website, Safe 2 Tell Colorado is a "statewide anonymous reporting tool available 24-hours a day to accept reports whenever a Colorado youth or concerned adult perceived a threat to their safety or the safety of others."[212] Calls are answered at a Colorado State Patrol communication center along with reporting capabilities on the internet and a mobile app. As reports come in, they are

153

immediately forwarded to local school officials and law enforcement agencies. After being reported, every incident is investigated by school and law enforcement agencies, action is in fact taken, and outcomes are tracked. The assurance that calls are not traced back to the reporting individual and that appropriate action is taken establishes the trust needed to persuade young people to move away from a code of silence and to take a stand.[213]

With all the wasted money by our local, state, and federal politicians, why can't we manage to put together a federal program like Safe 2 Tell Colorado? Isn't this program simple enough to where even politicians couldn't screw it up? I'll tell you why it's not being done nationwide — corruption and misuse of funds. As much as we need it, I'm not very optimistic to think that we could ask Washington D.C. to create a new program without them creating a whole new bureaucratic arm of the federal government that becomes another money laundering scam like most of the money they tax away from Americans. I realize many of our states are just as corrupt, but maybe we need to just try this at the state level where it's a little more controllable? I'd get behind any program like this where money was properly spent and books could be audited. I think it's a brilliant idea and one that could save many lives while also helping to mitigate future dangerous situations. Stopping one potentially bad decision by a young person could be the thing that redirects them and changes their entire life. We are complete failures if we can't see the value in something like this and find a way to do something similar for the sake of our kids.

MORE EMPHASIS ON SIDE EFFECTS OF DRUGS

Parents and patients have a right to know what the dangers and side effects of psychiatric drugs given to their children are and how they can affect a young person's developing brain. As pointed out in Chapter 6, these drugs can indeed rewire a child's maturing brain even as late as in their 20's. So, why do so many parents step aside and let teachers and physicians administer these mind-altering drugs without so much as an explanation of the negative side affects, not to mention the FDA's own black box warnings on them?

According to the CDC, most school-aged children's parents are in their 20's and early 30's.[214] While younger adults may seem to think they've seen it all by the time they're raising a child, they haven't. And oftentimes they lack the knowledge or even confidence to question professionals in various positions of authority. Many times parents tend to become intimidated and even overwhelmed with discussions about medicine, especially with their own or their kids' doctors. It's important to gain confidence to the point where a parent feels more prepared questioning doctors when it comes to their children's safety and well being. When prescriptions for these types of drugs are suggested, parents should be asking:

- Why does my child need this medicine and what symptoms will it help with?

- What potential side effects can occur if they take this medication?

- Is this the only medication available to treat his/her symptoms?

- When can he/she stop taking this medication?

- How often does he/she need to come in for monitoring during use?

- What alternative treatments are there that we can try before the medication?

While clearly something has to be done with it being okay for just any unqualified physician from any discipline being able to prescribe any drug that they aren't thoroughly educated or trained to prescribe, it's possible that even mental health professionals may need to receive a little more in-depth and detailed bit of education on the negative side effects of psychiatric drugs. If just a handful of side effects are taught in medical school as topics for a random pop quiz, that's not enough! I've personally sat in an office with a psychiatrist prescribing some of the very drugs discussed in this book — ones that have black box FDA warning labels on them — to an 11 year old child and not once did he even hint at any negative side effects of those medications nor was it mentioned that some of the medications had these FDA warning labels on them. I don't doubt that this particular doctor knew what he was doing or what he was talking about and he's probably really good at his job, but those warning labels aren't just there for his reading pleasure. They're also there for the patients — or the patients' parents — to know what chemicals they may be putting into their bodies and the harmful side effects they could potentially expect as a result.

I know the vast majority of physicians are good and decent people and that they honestly want what's best for their patients. I truly feel that if a percentage of them knew a little bit more about withdrawal side effects, as well as those other side effects common while taking the medications, that they'd entertain other possible therapies or at least keep a closer watch on their younger patients who are on these psychiatric medications. This is common sense. I don't need a medical degree to know this.

STOP ENCOURAGING SINGLE PARENT HOMES

This one's going to hurt some feelings. Tough. It's time that baby-making for money stops being a full time profession. The United States welfare system was either mistakingly designed to incentivize women to have as many kids as they could spit out, to remain unemployed or barely employed, and to stay single — or else the system was designed that way on purpose. If it was accidentally designed this way, then once again we have concrete evidence that the government couldn't stand on a beach and throw a rock into the ocean without hitting the desert instead. However, if this system was designed this way on purpose, then we have all the evidence we need that the U.S. government will go to any length to control the U.S. population by giving them free taxpayer money in exchange for votes and unquestioning compliance.

| *She actually makes $282 less a year by taking the job paying $40,000 more per year!* |

I once read an incredible example that laid out in understandable terms the incentive to rack up lots of government benefits by accepting a much lower paying job versus a much higher paying job. It showed that the single mom with two young children is better off settling for a job making only $29,000 per year because she will take home an annual total of $57,327 in pay after taxes when you add in her government handouts as opposed to her taking a much higher paying job of $69,000 per year because after taxes and with her much lower government handouts, she only takes home a grand total of $57,045.[215] She actually makes $282 *less* a year by taking the job paying $40,000 *more* per year! And you know a job paying $40,000 less per year has got to be much easier and have much less responsibly So, unless you happen to be a wiser person with the vision to see the bigger picture and avoid this obvious societal trap, you will be a willful slave to the system without any other choice but to remain in it and bang out more kids.

Unless we return to the days when a person hustled to find a job to help his family out instead of where we are today where a young man is bullied for walking to work in his McDonald's uniform shirt, we will never correct this cultural trap of dependency that only does more to keep a solid family unit from developing. Our young people are the ones suffering from this the most. As parents, we have to provide a better example for our kids or else all we're doing is showing them the way to be dependent and have no voice or real freedom to speak of.

SECURE OUR SCHOOLS LIKE WE DO CONGRESS

There are 535 total members of Congress in Washington D.C. These are the disconnected people with very little life experience in an actual real world setting who make our laws. It's sad, but that's just how it works out. To protect those 535 people and the 2 square miles that they operate within, the United States taxpayers pay to employ 2,300 officers in what's called the Capitol Police. You heard right, 2,300 officers are assigned to protect 535 people — in a 2 square mile area. That a ratio of over 4 police officers for every one congressperson. In fairness, I realize they don't all work at the same time. But even if 25% of the staff works at one time that's still at least one officer for every bloodsucking politician.

| *The budget for the Capitol Police (protecting Congress) in 2021 was $516 million.* |

159

Since all of those officers work within a 2 square mile area it should be pretty cheap, right? Not so fast. The budget for the Capitol Police in 2021 was $516 million[216] with a 7.4% annual increase realized each year since 2000. The budget for these guys to protect our elitist politicians is more than the budgets of Atlanta and Detroit according to the Cato Institute.[217] On top of this half a trillion dollars to protect 535 people within a couple of blocks, members of Congress also receive additional pass through privileges to pay for additional personal security outside of that little 2 mile area.

So for every one of the 535 elected officials in Washington D.C., we employ roughly 4 law enforcement personal and spend $964,485 a year — per elected official. It's probably safe to say that if we then add the pass through expenditures from each individual member, we tax payers are likely on the hook for over $1 million per year for each one of those self-righteous, pompous "public servants" who routinely talk down to us little ol' regular people like you and I. Unreal. You know why rampage killers don't attack members of congress at the U.S. Capitol? It's simple: they have a $516 million annual security budget.

But since members of Congress seem so concerned about children when they're in front of cameras after a rampage killing at a school, surely they allocate a pretty sizable sum of money to protect those children in schools, right?

Nope.

- THE ANTI-GUN CULTURE IS TORN

The anti-gun enterprise and its trendy followers —
including the massive teachers unions that pay loads of
money to anti-gun politicians — face a conundrum when it
comes to protecting our children in school versus protecting
adults in Congress. They're perfectly okay with most
government overreach and spending, just like they're okay
with a $516 million price tag to "protect" members of
Congress. But they are offended if we suggest the identical
methods to protect our defenseless children in schools.
They are very open about not "hardening" schools nor
placing trained personnel with firearms in our schools to
protect our children's lives. So what ideas are they bringing
to the table? When you read each of the following I want
you to immediately ask yourself, "How can this stop a
person from making the decision to shoot children and
acting on it?"

• Outlawing private guns sales: We have universal
  background checks. We've had them for *decades*. But
  what they mean is outlawing private gun sales. Don't ask
  me how these people think that not allowing private gun
  sales or gifts among family members or friends would
  stop even *one* of the school rampage killings in recent
  history. Not one of the school attacks that have taken
  place would've been prevented by what they call
  "universal background checks".

161

- Gun confiscation without due process: Extreme Risk Protection Orders (ERPOS), also known as "red flag gun laws", provide for *anyone* to petition law enforcement to remove a person's legally obtained firearms from them without providing them due process per the Constitution. This means that a disgruntled employee, a wronged ex-husband or wife, an angry neighbor, or even a criminal wanting to break into a particular home can report that a person threatened to kill them and that they are a danger to themselves or others. While many ERPOs do contain due process for minor threats (whatever that means), they all contain a more severe stage of the ERPO where the person is viewed as more of a serious threat and absolutely *no* due process is afforded the free American being accused, and his door can be kicked in and his firearms confiscated in the dead of the night. If we could without questions prove future crimes, this would be an awesome law. *But we can't.* Our Constitution does not allow Americans who have committed *no crimes* to have their Constitutional rights violated based on a hunch.

- Enact gun storage laws: I'm a huge proponent of teaching children and all family members the true dangers of playing with firearms and not taking the dangers of misuse seriously. I also encourage gun owners to "read the room" when it comes to who lives in their homes. If you need a gun safe because you don't think the inhabitants of your home can act responsibly around your firearms, then you have an educating and discipline problem to handle up on. And if you need to lock your guns up until everyone can be trusted, do it. But asking the government to force Americans to do things in their own homes is a path none of us want to go down. Once you give the federal government permission to do something they can't constitutionally do now, then they will take all future opportunities to violate those same privacy rights. Additionally, the irony is not lost on me when these people encourage gun storage laws, but then cite the fact that arming teachers is a bad idea because kids will steal the guns from teachers who improperly store them. So, you're saying some people don't follow or ignore laws?

- Raise the age to purchase semi-autos to 21: Not allowing adults under the age of 21 to purchase firearms to protect themselves and their families is a direct violation of the Second Amendment. As long as political parties promote allowing 16 year old kids to vote in local, state, and national elections because they're now so mature that they can pick this country's "leaders" who in turn make laws, then I won't even listen to their other argument that people under 21 now aren't mature enough to purchase and own firearms. All hypocrites suck.

- Establish threat assessment programs: The idea is to intervene and attempt to connect with children in school who seem disconnected and not right. I agree with and support this idea. Sadly, teachers and administrators are known to look the other way and even take part in

163

bullying at schools. (See Chapter 4) In fact, Nikolas Cruz gave off countless signs of disconnect and was even expelled. On a more peculiar note, you don't need government permission or additional funding to assemble threat assessment programs, *so do it already*!

- Create safe and equitable schools: This one is hilarious and an absolutely proven failure. The general idea is to punish students less who have done wrong and to make them feel better about themselves. This approach is *exactly* what got 17 people killed at Marjory Stoneman Douglas High School. Nikolas Cruz was a direct product of President Barack Obama and Eric Holder's PROMISE Program where local law enforcement would give offenders essentially glorified detention rather than having them arrested for criminal offenses. In return for looking the other way, local law enforcement received bribe money in the way of federal grants.

These ideas — clearly politically driven — do nothing for stopping humans from wanting to murder other humans. Although a good concept, even the threat assessment idea is worthless within the current government run education system. And not one of these ideas seeks out the actual cause of rampage killers. None of these ideas can be taken seriously as long as the individuals proposing them aren't serious about finding the actual root cause of rampage killers. Hopefully they all buy a copy of my book.

- NONE OF US WANT SCARED, UNPREPARED TEACHERS WITH GUNS

There is a foolish misconception that when concerned parents discuss arming educators that somehow the goal is to force firearms into every little timid, frightened, unfit and untrained teacher shuffling their feet lazily about the halls of every school in America.

A very small percentage of the teachers who don't want armed security in our schools most likely are just afraid of the presence of firearms and just being around them. That's pretty common with people who are ignorant about guns and gun owners, especially when they hear people talk about allowing some educators to be armed in schools. My guess is they're intimidated by guns since they have no knowledge of them and are afraid that they'll be expected or forced to carry a gun and they just aren't comfortable with doing that. Outside of being ignorant of the fact that other very well trained teachers may be very comfortable with that, I respect their apprehension and desire not to be armed. If there's one thing that we in the firearms community do well, it's to hold ourselves to a higher standard than those outside the community. Most of us would agree that if a person doesn't feel safe being in control of a firearm, we absolutely don't want them anywhere near one!

"There's nothing that a gun could have done in those six minutes..."

But sadly, many of these inadequate teachers never waste an opportunity to politicize a topic and instead of realizing the obvious — that trained people with firearms in a school are a very effective line of defense for them and school children — they repeat idiotic talking points that they've been given. In one instance, a teacher at Marjory Stoneman Douglas in Parkland who obviously had no working knowledge of firearms, believed that armed teachers would not have made any difference in stopping Nikolas Cruz's rampage killing on Feb. 14 2018. "There's nothing that a gun could have done in those six minutes ... a handgun would not have been any match for an AR-15, which is a weapon of war. They're not equal."[218] There's undoubtedly nothing that would have been done by *her* if she'd have been armed, but clearly any trained monkey could've saved many children's lives by ending Cruz's rampage with one well-placed pistol round as he awkwardly stumbled about the school firing aimlessly into doorways and windows. By making a statement as factually incorrect and downright stupid as she did, there's no doubt this teacher shouldn't be trusted with a loaded gun of any kind. I wonder if anyone's ever told her how ignorant her entire statement was. The one thing we must do when arming the appropriate persons in schools is to weed out all cowards and only allow qualified and capable people to be armed.

Randi Weingarten, president of the American Federation of Teachers, once said, "The one thing we do know doesn't work is when there is simply a reflex to harden schools and arm people so there will be catastrophe in a school in the event of a really terrible situation."[219] Really? How does she know that hardening a school with metal detectors and arming well-trained individuals with firearms will somehow result in a "catastrophe" in a school? This is simply posturing and politics from a person receiving big favors from a political party that her organization dumps a lot of membership money into. I understand the personal fear that Ms. Weingarten feels about guns. If I had no experience or knowledge about guns, I might feel the same way. But you can bet that if Ms. Weingarten had been in that school when Nikolas Cruz stormed in shooting that she would have begged for me to be at her side to end the "catastrophe" with my firearm and protect her life.

I'm definitely in favor of not allowing all teachers to be armed. In fact, I think any teacher wishing to carry a firearm in school around children should receive rigorous training, a strict mental evaluation, and bi-annual recertification.

Personally, I'd prefer we harden our school entrances and hire full time security guards that are trained in spotting depressed kids, bullied kids, possible abuse from home, drug use, and sexual abuse. Then train these men and women *heavily* how to take down attackers utilizing both non-lethal and lethal tactics. This may not totally eliminate rampage killers, but it would keep them out of our schools!

- METAL DETECTORS MIGHT HURT FEELINGS

Finally, National Education Association Vice-President Becky Pringle once stated, "we cannot convert our schools into prisons and treat our students like prisoners."[220] Hey, Becky, ask any student who hasn't been coached if he or she would rather have their classroom secured so they won't be murdered sitting at their desks or would they rather feel good about their incredibly pleasant surroundings while giving up any chance of being protected from murderers off the street. We know the answer. Becky's comment is remarkably stupid and an incredible instance of misguided conjecture. Securing the building our children go to school in in order to protect their lives no more makes them "prisoners" than does securing members of Congress' offices with a $516 million security budget makes *them* prisoners. Why don't we protect our children like we do members of Congress?

Answer me this: How can you be okay with Congress receiving $516 million dollars per year to have metal detectors and trained officers with firearms protecting them, but you aren't okay with, at the very least, the same amount of protection for our children in schools? Explain that to me or shut up. I don't listen to the "reasoning" of ignorant fools and hypocrites driven by political objectives.

CHAPTER 16: WHY NOTHING WILL CHANGE

"The state must declare the child to be the most precious treasure of the people. As long as the government is perceived as working for the benefit of the children, the people will happily endure almost any curtailment of liberty and almost any deprivation." — *Adolf Hitler*

I feel like every American who reads this book who doesn't have a vested interest in the big business of rampage killings likely have done and will continue to do their part in recognizing, reporting, and working toward helping our young people in their formative years to possibly prevent a rampage killing. But does everyone really want rampage killings to stop?

THE CONSTITUTION CAN'T BE CHANGED OVERNIGHT

In a weak attempt to make their point that the Constitution can be ignored on a whim, the anti-gun enterprise and politicians use the same old, tired example that "you can't yell 'fire' in a crowded theatre" to refer to the First Amendment not being absolute. But, you actually *can* yell "fire" in a crowded movie theatre. You just can't *falsely* yell "fire" in a theatre with the intent to cause a panic, no matter how many people are in it. In 1919, Justice Oliver Wendell Holmes made the statement "The most stringent protection of free speech would not protect a man in falsely shouting fire in a theatre and causing a panic," in his opinion in the case of Schenck v. United States. In the decision in which the Court unanimously upheld a conviction under the Espionage Act for distribution of flyers opposed to the draft to draft-aged men. The flyers urged resistance to induction into the military and this could be seen as an attempt to obstruct the draft, which is a criminal offense.[221] He also stated the following:

"We admit that, in many places and in ordinary times, the defendants, in saying all that was said in the circular, would have been within their constitutional rights. But the character of every act depends upon the circumstances in which it is done."[222]

He went on to state:

"The question in every case is whether the words used are used in such circumstances and are of such a nature as to create a clear and present danger that they will bring about the substantive evils that Congress has a right to prevent. It is a question of proximity and degree."[223]

So, the incorrect argument that even the First Amendment doesn't recognize the right to free speech *all* the time, so then the same must apply to the Second Amendment is based on a common omission from Holmes' statement — the word "false." It's there for a reason: you can't *falsely* yell "fire" with the intent to start a panic. Using the same reasons Holmes used in terms of the First Amendment, it's also not legal to purchase a stolen gun, to use a gun to protect yourself while committing a crime, or to kill someone with a gun. Context and intent matter.

But fear not, commies, because you *can* change the Constitution! Unfortunately for those wanting to change it for the wrong reasons, it is unlikely to happen in our lifetime as long as there are still a good number of patriotic Americans living and breathing.

In order for an amendment proposed by Congress to be added to the United States Constitution, the proposed amendment language must be approved by a two-thirds vote of both houses of every state and then the proposed amendments must be ratified by three-fourths of the 50 states. If that takes place, the archivist of the United States proclaims it as a new amendment to the U.S. Constitution and it's then enacted. So, no matter how loud the anti-gun enterprise and politicians shout, the Second Amendment won't be changing any time soon without the appropriate steps.

DEATH BY FIREARMS IS BIG BUSINESS FOR SOME

As stated earlier in the book, the anti-gun enterprise is a very lucrative industry. These organizations haul in some big-time cash every year simply by promoting fear and manipulating statistics. For example, Everytown for Gun

Safety alone brings in $106 million annually[224], and there are a number of other anti-Second Amendment groups out there doing the same kind of work. That's not small money for what amounts to essentially an elite club full of people feigning outrage a few times a year and selling t-shirts and bumper stickers here and there.

But let's face it, most normal people would indeed have to be paid over-the-top, life-changing money and have very few job responsibilities in order to even consider working for an organization that openly claims to push for gun safety, but creates and promotes literally zero gun safety initiatives. You'd have to be willing to ignore your conscience or somehow convince yourself that what you're doing isn't just for the money — even though it is. What's disgusting and troubling is that the killing of innocent people by evil people who just happen to choose guns to kill is a tolerated — but valuable — marketing tool that's absolutely necessary for these organizations to exist.

Think of it this way: if a lucrative business is 100% based on bad things happening to other people so that they can, in turn, pretend to care and be enraged about it each time it happens, do you really think a person making six figures a year shipping a few t-shirts and bumper stickers out really wants it to end? Because in reality, if all murders of innocent people with firearms ended tomorrow and it never happened again, what would these people do for a living? Now, while I do think they're frauds with a business model that encourages fear based on lies, I don't believe they're such cold-hearted scam artists that they actually *want* children to be killed. I don't think they stand around the water cooler at work or chat in elevators about how much they wish someone would decide to kill kids at another school or church. I just can't make myself believe they're that disgusting of human beings. But I do think that they've conditioned themselves to view these innocent victims as numbers and subconsciously see them as a means to an end for their businesses to continue. I know, that sounds rough, but I don't care how it sounds if it applies to you.

| *Stoking fear by tapping in to an emotional dynamic that no one wants to ever have to experience is a very powerful motivator.* |

These companies don't make or manufacture anything. Sure, they sell $30 t-shirts, $60 sweatshirts, and even signs for $12, but fear of your innocent child being killed indiscriminately while in school or walking down the street is what they really sell that brings in the big bucks. Stoking fear by tapping in to an emotional dynamic that no one wants to ever have to experience is a very powerful motivator. Fear can make a person do some very irrational things. Fear can make a person write checks to other people who promise that they can protect your child, but don't.

I suppose one last benefit to creating a fraudulent gun safety organization where no actual gun safety initiatives are promoted is that the participants get to wallow in their own righteous glory at their high dollar fund raisers and rallies as the self-appointed champions of the ultimate in virtue signaling causes — it's for the children. Yay. You know, I sleep really well at night knowing that I actually try to protect innocent lives. Imagine trying to live with the lie that you're the glorious tip of the spear for protecting our children when in reality all you're doing is railing against law-abiding Americans who just want to protect their own children.

The reason I go to such great lengths to explain the hypocrisy of so many of these anti-gun organizations who do absolutely nothing to promote any real initiatives involving gun safety (banning guns is not gun safety) is because it's important to recognize who's doing the real work out there. I mention a few of the true champions of actual gun safety in this book, but there are hundreds — maybe thousands — throughout the U.S. who strive daily to push and promote a wide variety of gun safety/safe handling programs, child safety initiatives, hunter safety courses, home safety courses, safe storage initiatives, and even "active shooter" seminars to defend innocent lives against rampage killers. While these organizations do take donations in some cases, many don't. And most of the people teaching the classes and working with the families, single moms, and children are unpaid volunteers.

To deflect from their own racket, the anti-gun enterprise would have you believe that gun manufacturers who have been around for decades are equivalent to the Nicolas Cage character in the movie "Lord of War" — making huge profits off of selling guns to just about any crumb-snatching rat bastard who can scrounge up a handful of blood-soaked dollar bills. That is a provably false narrative from an industry that itself directly profits from innocent people being killed. I find this incredibly ironic coming from the true Profiteers of Death themselves.

GUESS WHO DOESN'T PROFIT FROM RAMPAGE KILLINGS

As of 2021[225], there are 54,305 people employed in the Guns & Ammunition Manufacturing industry in the United States. That number has increased on average by 3.7% over the five years between 2016 and 2021.[226] These hard-working people have raised families all across America and have been promoting comprehensive firearm safety for as long as I can remember.

| *... the gun industry probably makes less money when a rampage killing takes place than a small town paperboy does selling newspapers misinforming people about it.* |*

But the firearms industry doesn't operate with massive margins of profit like the anti-gun enterprise does. The unsupported claim that the firearms industry profits off of innocent people being killed is just plain ignorant if you're fluent in even the most remedial of reading and math. On average, when a firearm of any kind is sold, the manufacturer profits between 30% to 40% and the ammunition has a margin of about 12%. These are industry averages and are hardly "get rich" margins. To be honest, the gun industry probably makes less money when a rampage killing takes place than a small town paperboy does selling newspapers misinforming people about it.

Let's look at one of our subjects in this book, Devin Kelley. Kelley used a super scary-looking AR-15 for his murders and is alleged to have fired nearly 700 rounds to murder the 26 innocent people he made the conscious choice to kill on that horrible day in Texas. At the time this rampage killing took place, the Ruger AR-15 that he used was priced at around $799 and the 5.56 NATO ammunition he used would have run about $161 for all 700 rounds as it sold at that time for about $0.23/round. That means that the firearms manufacturer profited roughly $279 and the ammunition manufacturer profited about $19. The firearms industry's profit from the person who purchased the gun and ammunition was $298. While hardly being life-changing money, was that all profit? Nope.

The federal government levies an "excise tax" on the firearms industry on goods sold. This tax is called the Firearms and Ammunition Excise Tax or "FAET." The funds collected were originally meant to support conservation and shooting sports activities such as the national parks, wildlife conservation efforts and so on, but I'm willing to bet that an audit on how this money is spent would reveal that none of it is spent where it's supposed to. If today's federal government can call free day care "infrastructure", what's to keep them from calling pay increases to ATF employees "conservation"?

This FAET tax on our Second Amendment averages out to be around 10% based on the type of firearms and goods sold. So that $298 that we thought the firearms industry profited when Devin Kelley purchased an AR-15 and ammo is now just $268. Wow. Going to be some big time bonuses paid out with that hunk of cheese!

In comparison, the true profiteers off of rampage killings — our anti-gun friends — only need to get 11 people to pay the minimum donation amount of $25 to surpass that presumed profit by the gun industry of $268 per rampage killing. However, the highest donation amount selection on their website is $1,000, unless you enter in an even higher amount. Now, if we take that $106 million per year[227] that Bloomberg's Everytown For Gun Safety makes and divide that by 365 days in a year, we come up with $290,410 per day that they gross. So, since there are roughly only 3 rampage killings a year that the anti-gun enterprise gets whipped up about, it's more than fair to say that using our daily average of $290,410, they generate $871,230 per year off of the rampage killings. Now, even though we know their profit margins are much higher than 35%, to compare apples and apples I'm going to use that low percentage of profit from the gun industry which puts the gun haters making a paltry $304,930 per year off of rampage killings, or $101,644 per actual event — that's profit. Again, the gun industry profited $268 at best per event.

| After the Parkland, Florida rampage murders…
Everytown saw their number of small
donors rise from 70,000 to 375,000[228] |

Need more proof that the anti-gun enterprise profits more than anyone when there's a rampage killing? Immediately after the Parkland, Florida rampage murders, Bloomberg's Everytown saw their number of small donors rise from 70,000 to 375,000[229]. If the new 305,000 donors only chose the lowest $25 donation amount available, that would have been a $7.6 million payday for them. Someone got a good Christmas bonus that year.

IT'S NOT JUST THE ANTI-GUN ENTERPRISE

A lot of people wonder why the media — mostly print and television — have leaned so far left and have settled in to their new roles as full time "opinion entertainment" instead of journalism or news. No one disagrees with the fact that no one delivers news anymore — no one. But why has it come to that? Why has the profession of a true "journalist" become as rare as a blacksmith? It's not just because they suck at being unbiased. The biggest reason is because the delivery system has changed.

Instead of today's consumers of current events seeking out their content by reading it in print or watching television, we now have smart devices that deliver both in one small, easy to use device. Why bother with a print magazine or newspaper when you can read the same information on your iPhone on the toilet without having to carry bulky magazines or newspapers in with you? (Don't lie, you read on the crapper.) Why waste time sitting on the couch waiting for the "news" to come on when you can catch up at your own pace on your smart device while laying down with your kids at night? And an added benefit to the portability of these devices over print and television is that you get your news much faster. I can't count the times that something major popped up on my Facebook timeline, but when I go search for it on "news" websites or on TV, it's not being reported yet. So what do smart devices have to do with the biased and slanted views of media today?

| *In 2008, print newspaper employees made up 62% of news media jobs. By 2020, that had dropped to fewer than 36%.* |

Smart devices have squeezed advertising revenue from print and television *hard*. Less money means less employees. News media employment in the United States is down by 26% since 2008.[230] Print has taken the biggest hit. In 2008, print newspaper employees made up 62% of news media jobs. By 2020, that had dropped to fewer than 36%. Print media is also either a day or a month behind in delivering the news. We now live in a culture of instant gratification and it's rare that someone will wait a month for the September issue of Sports Illustrated to get dropped in their mailbox when they can just follow them on social media.

Television hasn't been immune to the drop in viewers either. Even with the coronavirus keeping more scared people at home these days, television is still taking a hit as Nielsen statistics show that the percentage of Americans who watched their televisions at least once a week declined from 92% in 2019 to 87% in 2021.[231] A 5% drop of viewers at a time when viewership was expected to go up instead is massive. And don't think advertisers haven't reminded these television outlets of this drop in viewership. With a drop in viewers comes a drop in advertising dollars. I even looked at trends prior to the virus since it presents a huge wildcard, and I found that between 2018 and 2019, primetime network viewership of adults had fallen by 35%.[232]

One last point on print media — you have to be able to read it. That's no joke. If you can't read, what use is a magazine or newspaper to you? Here's two interesting facts that show how pathetic government-run education is: 1) 43 million U.S. adults possess low literacy skills[233], and 2) People aged 15–44 in the U.S. spend 10 minutes or less per day reading. Some people don't read newspapers and magazines because they *can't!*

| *When reporting on "mass shootings"... they've begun to include all gang-related shootings, drug-related shootings, and even armed robberies.[234]* |

All this left-leaning tomfoolery amongst the remaining media outlets in order to wrestle eyeballs away from each other has evolved into one big, giant free-for-all. Eyeballs equal clicks which equal money. The only way to one-up the next guy out there is to be the first one with something to report — *right or wrong* — and to be far more sensational and controversial with the story. In order to make their stories more sensational, the anti-gun enterprise and its partners in the media have begun to lie and conflate the raw data they get before releasing it as "news." When reporting on "mass shootings" — as they call them — they've begun to include all gang-related shootings, drug-related shootings, and even armed robberies.[235] They even use justified shootings by law enforcement in those numbers! That is outright deception meant to exaggerate numbers in order to make people feel like the problem is worse than it is. They're manipulating the news to make it more sellable.

OUR FRIENDS IN THE SWAMP GET FAT

Remember our friends in the anti-gun enterprise that we discussed earlier with their $106 million annual cash haul? Well, they need someone to reward for doing their dirty work in Congress for them. During the 2016 campaign cycle, the anti-gun enterprise bankrolled their anti-gun politicians in D.C. with campaign contributions totaling $3 million[236]. Not bad, right? Well, the "fear of guns" business must be good because in just four short years that chunk of change jumped to $23.5 million in 2020[237].

181

| Bernie Sanders made more money in 2020 from the anti-gun enterprise than 52 Americans put together! |

The U.S. Census Bureau puts the annual real median personal income per working American at $35,977 in 2019.[238] When I looked at the annual contributions the anti-gun enterprise made to politicians in D.C., the 20th highest paid politician — Andy Kim (D) of New Jersey — still made a whopping $47,481. That's $11,504 more per year than the average American makes. Now, you wonder why these people lay it on so thick without ever trying to enact any actual change that doesn't include banning guns? The top recipient in 2020 was our leading socialist sympathizer, Bernie Sanders (D), who raked in a pretty sweet $1,871,666. Bernie made more money in 2020 from the anti-gun enterprise than 52 American families put together! No wonder he can afford all those high dollar homes![239]

Now to be fair, there are gun rights organizations who support the Constitution and the Second Amendment who also lobby for their cause. But compared to what Sanders raked in, the highest paid politician receiving money to support gun rights in 2020 was Martha McSally (R) of Arizona who was able to snag a nice $516,777 in campaign contributions. That's still awesome work if you can get it, but still well over $1 million short of Bernie's take.

If the threat of being shot with a firearm went away tomorrow, people would stop donating to the anti-gun enterprise which would then stop donating to the likes of Bernie Sanders. While I don't think Bernie and the anti-gun enterprise want to see children murdered by guns, I can assure you they don't go to bed at night and pray that the threat of being shot with a gun goes away. They also aren't committing any of their millions to research these killings like I've done in this book.

BIG PHARMA AND POLITICIANS STAND TO LOSE TOO MUCH

According to market research, the worldwide pharmaceutical market was valued at nearly $1.3 trillion in 2019.[240] In America alone, we spent $535 billion on prescription drugs in 2018, an increase of 50% since 2010.[241] With that much money being tossed around by one single industry, they tend to wield a good bit of power.

Remember those fat cats I discussed who profit from rampage killings? Well, our politicians and the media do quite well with checks from the pharmaceutical industry. A September 2018 article by Jacob Bell titled, "Pharma advertising in 2018: TV, midterms, and specialty drugs" explained that 187 TV commercials representing 70 prescription medications had aired almost half a million times since the start of 2018 to the tune of $2.8 billion in revenue to the network and cable companies.[242] Interestingly, The Kaiser Family Foundation found that of the 28% of the people who requested medication they'd viewed on a drug commercial on TV, 12% were successful in obtaining the prescription from their doctor.[243] That's not a bad haul considering there are 121 million TV homes in the United States.[244]

And legislators do pretty good, too. Both major political parties pretty much split the overall money with the total for pharmaceutical manufacturing lobbyist dollars topping out at $161,069,206. Wow! No wonder politicians don't care about which drugs are peddled and ignore the true root cause of rampage killers. When you start to wonder how politicians manage to become millionaires in Congress with an annual salary starting at $174,000, this kind of payout certainly helps to explain a lot.

HARDENING OUR SCHOOLS WOULD HURT THEIR INCOME

It was hard for me to write the line "hardening our schools would hurt their income", but that is indeed a fact, regardless of the difficulty by decent people to understand that twisted mindset. The anti-gun opportunists' fabricated reason that they don't want to secure our schools because children might feel like they're in a prison is as silly as saying putting pictures of bats up in classrooms around Halloween will make kids think they're Batman in the Bat Cave. It's just stupid and no one really believes that. It makes me wonder if the 100,000 fans who walk past hundreds of armed security guards at college football games every Saturday each fall think they're somehow magically transported to Guantanamo Bay?

One of the more hilarious yet ridiculous statements I've ever read against making our children safer by hardening schools was made by, apparently, a dope-smoking hippy who is the professor of education at UCLA and director of the Center for the Transformation of Schools, Pedro Noguera, where he made the flowery statement "the idea is that we're not safe simply because we have police officers with guns. We're safe because people respect the laws. We're safe because we respect each other. And we need to find ways to reinforce those bonds of solidarity in our society that allow us to live a safe and comfortable life."[245]

Hey Pedro, you know who doesn't respect laws? You know who doesn't respect you? You know who couldn't care less about your cute little safe and comfortable life? *Criminals and rampage killers!* While you're having some cotton candy love fest and dancing around in your mom's underwear picking daisies in a field full of unicorns singing Celine Dion songs, a rampage killer is kicking the unsecured front door of your school in ready to smoke any innocent soul who falsely believed all that idiotic, feel-good jibber-jabber that you just vomited out of your face hole.

| *"Security tends to actually make us feel more stressed and less able to relax when there are people around with guns who are patrolling."*[246] |

This guy went on to say, "Security tends to actually make us feel more stressed and less able to relax when there are people around with guns who are patrolling."[247] Wow. Apparently they don't drug test professors at UCLA. This guy thinks children will feel *less* safe with armed security personnel protecting their lives. Apparently the bar is pretty low for education "leaders" in the state with a bear on its flag.

You know what type of place *is* secured like a prison that doesn't have a single gun-related death within its grounds? *A prison!* I bet if we built a school behind prison walls that was apart from the inmates, every single anti-gun parent in the country would send their kids to that school, including ol' Pedro here. You see, this is what we're up against. These people and their dangerous, feel-good logic are proof that a bunch of handsomely framed degrees on a person's wall is only indicative of how much schooling they've had, not proof of intelligence.

Let's apply our "5 Whys" exercise to further demonstrate the idiocy of politicians and the anti-gun enterprise who don't want to harden schools to protect our children:

FIRST WHY: "Why don't you want to harden our schools?"
ANSWER: "Because children won't feel safe."

SECOND WHY: "Why wouldn't children feel safe?"
ANSWER: "Because people will have guns."

THIRD WHY: "What people will have guns?"
ANSWER: "The ones protecting the children."

RULES FOR THEE, NOT FOR ME

No one is surprised when examples of hypocrisy come from Washington D.C. In fact, good luck finding anyone with more than a single digit IQ who believes legislation passed by Congress actually applies to its members. But "school choice" is a bothersome one for me.

| *...a vote to allow children in dangerous school districts to attend a school of choice failed, with 57 members who exercise school choice for their own children voting against the amendment.* |

Most Americans see the choice to send their children to the best schools possible for them as a fundamental choice to be made in order for them to receive the best education possible. But many members of Congress don't see it that way — at least not for *your* children. Researchers at The Heritage Foundation conducted a survey of Members of Congress on school choice. Not all members responded to the survey, but for those who did, the survey found that members of the House and Senate who serve on the actual committees that have jurisdiction over educational issues were the most likely to send their children to private schools instead of public schools with a whopping 61% of Senate Finance Committee members and 57% of Senate Health, Education, Labor, and Pensions Committee members admitting that they send their children to private school.[248] In one example, a vote to allow children in dangerous school districts to attend a school of choice failed, with 57 members who exercise school choice *for their own children* voting against the amendment. [249]

Is this hypocrisy by lawmakers just so that their children will receive a better education than that of most of the taxpayers like you and I? Doubtful. Five of the top elite private schools in the Washington D.C. area that some politicians send their own children to charge tuition rates of $36,730 a year to as much as $45,440 a year. Rest assured that not only are these prestigious schools not located right in the middle of troubled areas of the community, but they are well protected. When have you ever heard of a rampage killing at Sidwell Friends School, Georgetown Day School, National Cathedral School, Maret School, or The Potomac School in Washington D.C.? Never. In fact, we all know how insanely deadly the Chicago area is with an average shooting of 80 to 100 instances a week, right.[250] But not once have we ever heard of a single case of even so much as a gun on campus at the prestigious University of Chicago Lab School, a private PK-12 school associated with the University of Chicago that the Obama family's girls attended prior to his presidency.[251] With the level of out of control violence in that city, I don't even have to ask if the school is well protected.

Politicians have rarely been viewed favorably in this country and it's mostly because of the level of hypocrisy that they pretend doesn't exist. Let's face it — your children are expendable to them. And if you can stomach a certain amount of brutal truth, your kids are collateral damage to the anti-gun politicians and the anti-gun enterprise. As long as some kids continue to get murdered so that they can put on a long face and shed some fake tears, the money keeps rolling in. Now, as I've said before, I'm not suggesting that they *want* your kids to die in a "school shooting" in order to keep their anti-gun wish list alive, but they certainly aren't doing a darn thing at the legislative level to indicate to me that my son's life means as much as theirs does. I will go to my grave thinking that of them.

CHAPTER 17: WHY I CARE

"It is easier to build strong children than to repair broken men." — Frederick Douglass

The world we live in today screams out for some sense of logic and reason to be applied in the midst of all the unconditional craziness. At times, it feels like a drunk is recklessly driving a car down the road of life and none of us sane people can seem to get out of it. The screams for logic and reason are ultimately drowned out by the celebration of virtue-signaling, chest-beating underachievers with little to offer anyone.

Today, we are expected to believe that it's acceptable for grown men with male genitalia to be naked, inches away from our young daughters in public restrooms that we as fathers can't go into. We are expected to believe that the color of our skin at the time of our birth is a determining factor as to whether or not we are racist. We are expected to believe that it's acceptable for law enforcement to illegally enter our homes, illegally search them, and illegally remove items from them that we legally purchased and possess, without due process per the Constitution.

These things are unacceptable to me and most Americans across the country. Politicians and the media want to convince you that you are the minority if you don't agree with them — but *you are not*. These entities are motivated by profit and control and they have everything to gain from a divisive, distrustful populous. *They* are the minority, not us.

So when most of us honest, hard-working Americans feel the constant, steady push to attack not only the Second Amendment, but all rights enshrined by our founding fathers in the Constitution, it ignites a fire in us that can't be extinguished by attempting to shame us into thinking that we're somehow the problem for not falling in lockstep with the group-thinking community.

I WON'T SURRENDER MY GUNS TO THESE NUTJOBS

I wrote this book out of necessity and the frustration that no one else would write it. I've watched over the years when there's a rampage killing where no one points out the obvious or even inquires about it. Sure, the media blasts headlines asking what the cause of rampage killings is, but then they go on to incorrectly answer their own question and it's always an uninformed swipe at guns and gun owners. When Americans are faced with a relentless attack on our gun rights by an overtly corrupt, power hungry consortium like we face today, we will not willingly surrender the very guns meant to protect ourselves and our families just because that group feigns outrage after a rampage killing. If we've broken no Constitutional laws, then we've done nothing to justify being disarmed, especially based on false pretenses. To be clear, *the existence of firearms is 100% not the reason for rampage killings*. "Access to guns" is not the reason for rampage killings. Certain types of guns are not the reason for rampage killings. *The existence and evolution of rampage killers is the reason for rampage killings* and I proved it in this book.

WHO SUFFERS FROM THIS DISINGENUOUS APPROACH?

When rampage killings are politicized and the search for the true root cause of them never happens, the effects are widespread and never ending. When we ignore the root cause of rampage killings we not only put future victims in danger, but we willfully give up on all of those young people who may need our help escaping the "Devil's Triangle."

As adults, we're expected to be wiser due to life experiences that help guide us in making better decisions and picking up on various signs of danger in life. On the other hand, we can't expect most children to feel confident enough to seek outside help when they're being abused by a parent or family member. They're thinking, "I'm family — this must be normal." We can't expect a teenager to know when they're being manipulated or used by a peer. They're thinking, "They're my friend — they wouldn't do anything to trick or hurt me." We can't expect a young person to push back when a doctor nonchalantly prescribes psychiatric drugs that are potentially harmful to them. They're thinking, "They have a medical degree — I should just do whatever they say." We are the voices for these young people and it is our responsibility to protest and speak up for them when we see those pretending to care about them doing nothing to ensure their safety.

IT'S OKAY TO RAISE YOUR BOYS TO BE MEN

From 1982 to 2021, 97% of rampage shooters in the United States were male.[252]And if we look at 27 of the most recent rampage killings in America, 26 of them were committed by males without their fathers in the home.[253]Maybe it's just a coincidence, but it almost appears that there may be something to this fatherless home thing. *(Was my sarcasm as obvious as I tried to make it?)*

To be clear, this is not a conversation about one parent being more important than the other. Both parents in most households contribute immensely to a child's upbringing, and in most cases, mothers are very present — thank God for that. But we cannot deny the impact a father has on his son's development. A father more effectively raises a boy to be a man and good men grow up to be good fathers. A good father does everything from dropping the hammer on his son when he gets out of line to teaching him how to treat his mother, other women, and other people with respect. And judging by the lack of respect in America today, I'd say the lack of fathers in the home is a doggone epidemic!

I'd like to point out that the father figure in the home doesn't necessarily have to be the boy's *biological* father either. If the biological father is garbage, it's best to not have him in the picture anyway. But that doesn't mean another man — a step dad, a grandfather, an uncle, a boyfriend — can't step into that "father figure" role and deal some life lessons to a young man needing some positive influence and direction.

Society today has a direct influence on parents and children while at the same time being a direct result of the failings of parenting efforts. Somewhere along the line it became trendy to not teach boys to be strong and confident. It became trendy to not teach boys to open doors for women. It became trendy for boys to be soft and overly passive. As a result, we have a bunch of disrespectful, delicate, whiny, pansies who have the chromosomes of actual men, but are complete anomalies who are scared of their own shadows. It's downright embarrassing to see some of the types of "men" this society is producing today. A strong, caring father in many cases can be the difference maker.

And even though girls only account for 3% of rampage killings, studies show that daughters are less likely to engage in problematic behavior when they have a positive relationship with their fathers.[254] It sure seems like all of the available data we have points to the fact that having a positive father figure around plays a major role in young people developing into positive members of society. Sadly, the media is more focused on tearing down the traditional family unit and today's politicians are more than happy to help them with this by taxing the traditional home out of existence.

WE HAVE TO DO BETTER

As a staunch gun rights advocate, I'm committed to protecting my Second Amendment rights. And as a father, I'm committed to protecting my family while striving to make the world a safer place to live for all children. It is absolutely possible to do all of this at the same time. I know that our future is only as good as the mental state of our children. This is an undeniable fact.

We cannot wait until after we've abandoned our responsibilities as parents — or worse, contributed to the problem — to try to fix or salvage what's left of our broken children. The world presents enough challenges to our young people today without us making it harder for them. Of all the causal factors I mention in this book that can negatively impact a young person, we are without a doubt the most important one that can have the most positive and longest-lasting effect on them.

The amount of love and respect we show our children in their formative years has the ability to shape them into leaders of the future instead of its rampage killers. What we do today shapes our children tomorrow.

Second Amendment

A well regulated militia, being necessary to the security of a free state, the right of the people to keep and bear arms, shall not be infringed.

[1] Brian Schwartz, "Bloomberg's huge donation helps his gun safety group raise record revenue in 2018", CNBC, November 26, 2019 https://www.cnbc.com/2019/11/26/bloomberg-vs-nra-huge-donation-lifts-gun-safety-groups-revenue.html

[2] Sandi Leyva, "How Does Your Revenue Stack Up to Other Small Businesses?", Quick Books, March 13, 2015 https://quickbooks.intuit.com/r/money/how-does-your-revenue-stack-up-to-other-small-businesses/

[3] Joe Bartozzi, "Guns Are Selling, But Gun Safety Is Priceless", NSSF, July 7, 2020 https://www.nssf.org/articles/guns-are-selling-but-gun-safety-is-priceless/

[4] Josiah Bates, "What Counts as a Mass Shooting? Why So Much of America's Gun Violence Gets Overlooked", Time, March 30, 2021 https://time.com/5947893/what-constitutes-a-mass-shooting/

[5] Hady Mawajdeh, "Why Some Shootings Are Called Mass Shootings And Others Are Ignored", November 13, 2019 https://wamu.org/story/19/11/13/why-some-shootings-are-called-mass-shootings-and-others-are-ignored/

[6] James Densley and Jillian Peterson, "Opinion: We analyzed 53 years of mass shooting data. Attacks aren't just increasing, they're getting deadlier" September 1, 2019 https://www.latimes.com/opinion/story/2019-09-01/mass-shooting-data-odessa-midland-increase

[7] John R. Lott, Jr., 'Gun Control Myths", 81

[8] Lily Rothman, "How the Son of Sam Serial Killer Was Finally Caught", Time, August 10, 2015 https://time.com/3979004/son-of-sam-caught/

[9] Scott A. Bonn Ph.D., "The Differences Between Psychopaths and Sociopaths", Psychology Today, January 9, 2018, https://psychologytoday.com/us/blog/wicked-deeds/201801/the-differences-between-psychopaths-and-sociapaths

[10] "What are Personality Disorders?" https://www.psychiatry.org/patients-families/personality-disorders/what-are-personality-disorders

[11] James Fallon, "The Psychopath Inside", 57

[12] James Fallon, "The Psychopath Inside", 57

[13] American Psychiatric Association, "Diagnostic And Statistical Manual Of Mental Disorders", 657

[14] American Psychiatric Association, "Diagnostic And Statistical Manual Of Mental Disorders", 657

[15] Kendra Cherry, "What Is Antisocial Personality Disorder (ASPD)?" July 24, 2020 https://www.verywellmind.com/antisocial-personality-disorder-2795566

[16] American Psychiatric Association, "Diagnostic And Statistical Manual of Mental Disorders", 659

[17] Scott A. Bonn Ph.D., "The Differences Between Psychopaths and Sociopaths", Psychology Today, January 9, 2018, https://psychologytoday.com/us/blog/wicked-deeds/201801/the-differences-between-psychopaths-and-sociapaths

[18] James Alan Fox/Jack Levin/Emma E. Fridel, "Extreme Killing: Understanding Serial and Mass Murder", 45

[19] Marcia Purse, "How Sociopaths Are Different from Psychopaths", Very Well Mind, June 15, 2020 https://www.verywellmind.com/what-is-a-sociopath-380184

[20] Marcia Purse, "How Sociopaths Are Different from Psychopaths" June 15, 2020 https://www.verywellmind.com/what-is-a-sociopath-380184

[21] American Psychiatric Association, "Diagnostic And Statistical Manual Of Mental Disorders", 657

[22] https://www.cdc.gov/nchs/data/databriefs/db395-tables-508.pdf#page=4

[23] https://www.cdc.gov/nchs/data/databriefs/db395-tables-508.pdf#page=4

[24] Ray Sipherd, "The third-leading cause of death in US most doctors don't want you to know about", February 22, 2018 https://www.cnbc.com/2018/02/22/medical-errors-third-leading-cause-of-death-in-america.html

[25] https://www.cdc.gov/nchs/data/databriefs/db395-tables-508.pdf#page=4

[26] https://www.cdc.gov/nchs/data/databriefs/db395-tables-508.pdf#page=4

[27] Drew Desilver, "Suicides account for most gun deaths", May 24, 2013 https://www.pewresearch.org/fact-tank/2013/05/24/suicides-account-for-most-gun-deaths/

[28] Cheryl Buehler and Kay Pasley, "Fatherlessness, Poverty, and Crime", United Families International, https://www.unitedfamilies.org/child-development/fatherlessness-poverty-and-crime/

[29] Kevin N. Wright, Ph.D., Karen E. Wright, M.S.W., Gerald (Jerry) P. Regier, "Family Life and Delinquency and Crime: A Policymakers' Guide to the Literature", U.S. Department of Justice National Institute of Justice, January 15, 1993, https://www.ojp.gov/pdffiles1/Digitization/140517NCJRS.pdf

[30] https://www.dictionary.com/browse/broken-home

[31] Jessica M. Solis, Julia M. Shadur, Alison R. Burns, and Andrea M. Hussong, "Understanding the Diverse Needs of Children whose Parents Abuse Substances", June 5, 2012 https://www.ncbi.nlm.nih.gov/pmc/articles/PMC3676900/

[32] Kathleen C. Basile, Ph.D., Kathryn Jones, M.S.W., Sharon G. Smith, Ph.D., Rape, Abuse & Incest National Network (RAINN) Staff, "Effects of domestic violence on children", Office on Women's Health, April 2, 2019 https://www.womenshealth.gov/relationships-and-safety/domestic-violence/effects-domestic-violence-children

[33] Vicki Larson, "How a Parent's Infidelity Can Hurt a Child", Huffpost, February 26, 2015 https://www.huffpost.com/entry/how-a-parents-infidelity-can-hurt-a-child_b_6751696

[34] Patrick Fagan, "The Real Root Causes of Violent Crime: The Breakdown of Marriage, Family, and Community", Heritage, March 17, 1995 https://www.heritage.org/crime-and-justice/report/the-real-root-causes-violent-crime-the-breakdown-marriage-family-and

[35] Emilie Kao, "The Crisis of Fatherless Shooters", Heritage, March 14, 2018 https://www.heritage.org/marriage-and-family/commentary/the-crisis-fatherless-shooters

[36] Doreen Huschek, Catrien Bijleveld, "Parental criminality and children's family-life trajectories: Findings for a mid-20th century cohort", Longitudinal and Life Course Studies 2015 Volume 6 Issue 4 Pp 379

[37] Emilie Kao, "The Crisis of Fatherless Shooters", Heritage, March 14, 2018 https://www.heritage.org/marriage-and-family/commentary/the-crisis-fatherless-shooters

[38] Economic & Social Research Council, "Children, brain development and the criminal law", Science Daily, June 18, 2012 https://www.sciencedaily.com/releases/2012/06/120618102840.htm

[39] Kevin N. Wright, Ph.D., Karen E. Wright, M.S.W., Gerald (Jerry) P. Regier, "Family Life and Delinquency and Crime: A Policymakers' Guide to the Literature", U.S. Department of Justice National Institute of Justice, January 15, 1993, https://www.ojp.gov/pdffiles1/Digitization/140517NCJRS.pdf

[40] Patrick Fagan, "The Breakdown of Marriage, Family, and Community", Heritage, March 17, 1995 https://www.heritage.org/crime-and-justice/report/the-real-root-causes-violent-crime-the-breakdown-marriage-family-and

[41] Patrick Fagan, "The Real Root Causes of Violent Crime: The Breakdown of Marriage, Family, and Community", Heritage, March 17, 1995 https://www.heritage.org/crime-and-justice/report/the-real-root-causes-violent-crime-the-breakdown-marriage-family-and

[42] Patrick Fagan, "The Real Root Causes of Violent Crime: The Breakdown of Marriage, Family, and Community", Heritage, March 17, 1995 https://www.heritage.org/crime-and-justice/report/the-real-root-causes-violent-crime-the-breakdown-marriage-family-and

[43] Cynthia C. Harper and Sara S. McLanahan, "Father Absence and Youth Incarceration," *Journal of Research on Adolescence* 14, (2004): 369-397.

[44] Patrick Fagan, "The Real Root Causes of Violent Crime: The Breakdown of Marriage, Family, and Community", Heritage, March 17, 1995 https://www.heritage.org/crime-and-justice/report/the-real-root-causes-violent-crime-the-breakdown-marriage-family-and

[45] Patrick Fagan, "The Real Root Causes of Violent Crime: The Breakdown of Marriage, Family, and Community", Heritage, March 17, 1995 https://www.heritage.org/crime-and-justice/report/the-real-root-causes-violent-crime-the-breakdown-marriage-family-and

[46] "36 Shocking Statistics on Fatherless Homes", October 4, 2018, https://lifeisbeautiful.org/statistics-on-fatherless-homes/

[47] "36 Shocking Statistics on Fatherless Homes", October 4, 2018, https://lifeisbeautiful.org/statistics-on-fatherless-homes/

[48] "36 Shocking Statistics on Fatherless Homes", October 4, 2018, https://lifeisbeautiful.org/statistics-on-fatherless-homes/

[49] "36 Shocking Statistics on Fatherless Homes", October 4, 2018, https://lifeisbeautiful.org/statistics-on-fatherless-homes/

[50] Patrick Fagan, "The Real Root Causes of Violent Crime: The Breakdown of Marriage, Family, and Community", Heritage, March 17, 1995 https://www.heritage.org/crime-and-justice/report/the-real-root-causes-violent-crime-the-breakdown-marriage-family-and

[51] Patrick Fagan, "The Real Root Causes of Violent Crime: The Breakdown of Marriage, Family, and Community", Heritage, March 17, 1995 https://www.heritage.org/crime-and-justice/report/the-real-root-causes-violent-crime-the-breakdown-marriage-family-and

[52] "What are marriage penalties and bonuses?", https://www.taxpolicycenter.org/briefing-book/what-are-marriage-penalties-and-bonuses

[53] Amy Morin, LCSW, "Bullying Statistics Everyone Should Know", Very Well Family, April 19, 2019 https://www.verywellfamily.com/bullying-statistics-to-know-4589438

[54] Becton Loveless, "Bullying Epidemic: Facts, Statistics and Prevention", Education Corner, https://www.educationcorner.com/bullying-facts-statistics-and-prevention.html

[55] Becton Loveless, "Bullying Epidemic: Facts, Statistics and Prevention", Education Corner, https://www.educationcorner.com/bullying-facts-statistics-and-prevention.html

[56] Amy Morin, LCSW, "Bullying Statistics Everyone Should Know", Very Well Family, April 19, 2019 https://www.verywellfamily.com/bullying-statistics-to-know-4589438

[57] Amy Morin, LCSW, "Bullying Statistics Everyone Should Know", Very Well Family, April 19, 2019 https://www.verywellfamily.com/bullying-statistics-to-know-4589438

[58] Amy Morin, LCSW, "Bullying Statistics Everyone Should Know", Very Well Family, April 19, 2019 https://www.verywellfamily.com/bullying-statistics-to-know-4589438

[59] Becton Loveless, "Bullying Epidemic: Facts, Statistics and Prevention", Education Corner, https://www.educationcorner.com/bullying-facts-statistics-and-prevention.html

[60] Becton Loveless, "Bullying Epidemic: Facts, Statistics and Prevention", Education Corner, https://www.educationcorner.com/bullying-facts-statistics-and-prevention.html

[61] Becton Loveless, "Bullying Epidemic: Facts, Statistics and Prevention", Education Corner, https://www.educationcorner.com/bullying-facts-statistics-and-prevention.html

[62] Becton Loveless, "Bullying Epidemic: Facts, Statistics and Prevention", Education Corner, https://www.educationcorner.com/bullying-facts-statistics-and-prevention.html

[63] "Zero Tolerance", https://supportiveschooldiscipline.org/zero-tolerance-policy

[64] Jessie Klein, "The Bully Society", 127

[65] "Facts About Bullying", August 12, 2020 https://www.stopbullying.gov/resources/facts

[66] Becton Loveless, "Bullying Epidemic: Facts, Statistics and Prevention", Education Corner, https://www.educationcorner.com/bullying-facts-statistics-and-prevention.html

[67] Jessie Klein, "If Cho had not been bullied ...", April 26, 2007 https://www.newsday.com/opinion/if-cho-had-not-been-bullied-1.573555

[68] Colleen Flaherty, "Educators share how No Child Left Behind has affected their classroom", February 20, 2015 https://educationvotes.nea.org/2015/02/20/educators-share-how-no-child-left-behind-has-affected-their-classroom/

[69] Marilyn Wedge Ph.D., "No Child Left Unmedicated", October 17, 2013 https://www.psychologytoday.com/us/blog/suffer-the-children/201310/no-child-left-unmedicated

[70] Kenneth Saltman, "Truthout: The ADHD Epidemic: Smart Drugs and the Control of Bodies and Minds", August 30, 2016 https://nepc.colorado.edu/blog/adhd-epidemic

[71] "Overdiagnosis: Schools Under Pressure on ADHD", May 9, 2014 https://www.rwjf.org/en/library/articles-and-news/2014/04/overdiagnosis--schools-under-pressure-on-adhd-.html

[72] "dexmethylphenidate Rx", https://reference.medscape.com/drug/focalin-xr-dexmethylphenidate-342996#5

[73] "dexmethylphenidate Rx", https://reference.medscape.com/drug/focalin-xr-dexmethylphenidate-342996#5

[74] "dexmethylphenidate Rx", https://reference.medscape.com/drug/focalin-xr-dexmethylphenidate-342996#5

[75] "dexmethylphenidate Rx", https://reference.medscape.com/drug/focalin-xr-dexmethylphenidate-342996#5

[76] "Children with ADHD at increased risk for depression and suicidal thoughts as adolescents", October 3, 2010 https://www.uchicagomedicine.org/forefront/news/children-with-adhd-at-increased-risk-for-depression-and-suicidal-thoughts-as-adolescents

[77] "New warnings on stimulants for ADHD: Cause for alarm?" October 5, 2006 https://www.mdedge.com/psychiatry/article/62370/neurology/new-warnings-stimulants-adhd-cause-alarm

[78] "Children with ADHD at increased risk for depression and suicidal thoughts as adolescents", October 3, 2010 https://www.uchicagomedicine.org/forefront/news/children-with-adhd-at-increased-risk-for-depression-and-suicidal-thoughts-as-adolescents

[79] Lyndsey Layton, "How Bill Gates pulled off the swift Common Core revolution", June 7, 2014 https://www.washingtonpost.com/politics/how-bill-gates-pulled-off-the-swift-common-core-revolution/2014/06/07/a830e32e-ec34-11e3-9f5c-9075d5508f0a_story.html

[80] Lyndsey Layton, "How Bill Gates pulled off the swift Common Core revolution", June 7, 2014 https://www.washingtonpost.com/politics/how-bill-gates-pulled-off-the-swift-common-core-revolution/2014/06/07/a830e32e-ec34-11e3-9f5c-9075d5508f0a_story.html

[81] Lyndsey Layton, "How Bill Gates pulled off the swift Common Core revolution", June 7, 2014 https://www.washingtonpost.com/politics/how-bill-gates-pulled-off-the-swift-common-core-revolution/2014/06/07/a830e32e-ec34-11e3-9f5c-9075d5508f0a_story.html

[82] 'Brain Development", https://www.firstthingsfirst.org/early-childhood-matters/brain-development/

[83] Stephen Johnson, "Why is 18 the age of adulthood if the brain can take 30 years to mature?", March 20, 2019, https://bigthink.com/mind-brain/adult-brain?rebelltitem=1#rebelltitem1

[84] Stephen Johnson, "Why is 18 the age of adulthood if the brain can take 30 years to mature?", March 20, 2019, https://bigthink.com/mind-brain/adult-brain?rebelltitem=1#rebelltitem1

[85] James Fallon, "The Psychopath Inside", 57

[86] Deborah Halber, "Motivation: Why You Do the Things You Do", https://www.brainfacts.org/thinking-sensing-and-behaving/learning-and-memory/2018/motivation-why-you-do-the-things-you-do-082818

[87] Dr. Bryan Bruno, Medical Director, "Serotonin and Dopamine: Getting to Know Your Neurotransmitters", January 4, 2020 https://www.midcitytms.com/serotonin-and-dopamine-getting-to-know-your-neurotransmitters/

[88] Fu-Ming Zhou, Yong Liang, Ramiro Salas, Lifen Zhang, Mariella De Biasi, and John A. Dani, "SSRI antidepressants involve dopamine as well as serotonin signaling", Neuron, April 6, 2005 https://www.eurekalert.org/pub_releases/2005-04/cp-sai040105.php

[89] Fu-Ming Zhou, Yong Liang, Ramiro Salas, Lifen Zhang, Mariella De Biasi, and John A. Dani, "SSRI antidepressants involve dopamine as well as serotonin signaling", Neuron, April 6, 2005 https://www.eurekalert.org/pub_releases/2005-04/cp-sai040105.php

[90] Vera Hassner Sharav, "Children in Clinical Research: A Conflict of Moral Values", December 7, 2010 https://www.tandfonline.com/doi/pdf/10.1162/152651603322781639

[91] M H Teicher, C Glod, J O Cole, "Emergence of intense suicidal preoccupation during fluoxetine treatment", February 1990 https://pubmed.ncbi.nlm.nih.gov/2301661/

[92] Joseph Glenmullen, MD, "Prozac: Pro and Con", June 2, 2000 https://www.webmd.com/depression/features/prozac-pro-con

[93] "Rise in Prescription Drug Misuse and Abuse Impacting Teens", https://www.samhsa.gov/homelessness-programs-resources/hpr-resources/rise-prescription-drug-misuse-abuse-impacting-teens

[94] Catherine Tom-Revzon, PharmD, Arnold & Marie Schwartz, Bernard Lee, PharmD, "Psychotropics in Children and Adolescents", https://www.uspharmacist.com/article/psychotropics-in-children-and-adolescents-11506

[95] Nicole Beurkens, "Taking a Stand: Educators and Medication Recommendations", May 11, 2015 https://www.drbeurkens.com/taking-a-stand-educators-and-medication-recommendations/

[96] John M. Grohol, Psy.D., "Antidepressants Overprescribed in Primary Care", August 8, 2011, https://psychcentral.com/blog/antidepressants-overprescribed-in-primary-care#1

[97] Amy Novotney, "Are preschoolers being overmedicated?", July/August 2015 https://www.apa.org/monitor/2015/07-08/preschoolers

[98] Nicole Beurkens, "Taking a Stand: Educators and Medication Recommendations", May 11, 2015 https://www.drbeurkens.com/taking-a-stand-educators-and-medication-recommendations/

[99] Joseph Glenmullen, MD, "Prozac: Pro and Con", June 2, 2000 https://www.webmd.com/depression/features/prozac-pro-con

[100] "School Shootings: Mental Health Watchdog Says Psychotropic Drug Use by School Shooters Merits Federal Investigation", February 21, 2018 https://www.prnewswire.com/news-releases/school-shootings-mental-health-watchdog-says-psychotropic-drug-use-by-school-shooters-merits-federal-investigation-300601826.html

[101] Thomas J. Moore, Joseph Glenmullen, Curt D. Furberg, "Prescription Drugs Associated with Reports of Violence Towards Others" December 15, 2010 https://www.ncbi.nlm.nih.gov/pmc/articles/PMC3002271/

[102] Thomas J. Moore, Joseph Glenmullen, Curt D. Furberg, "Prescription Drugs Associated with Reports of Violence Towards Others" December 15, 2010 https://www.ncbi.nlm.nih.gov/pmc/articles/PMC3002271/

[103] Todd Calder, "The Apparent Banality of Evil: The Relationship between Evil Acts and Evil Character", Journal of Social Philosophy, 2003 https://www.academia.edu/7364151/The_Apparent_Banality_of_Evil_The_Relationship_between_Evil_Acts_and_Evil_Character

[104] Emilie Kao, "The Crisis of Fatherless Shooters", Heritage, March 14, 2018 https://www.heritage.org/marriage-and-family/commentary/the-crisis-fatherless-shooters

[105] Becton Loveless, "Bullying Epidemic: Facts, Statistics and Prevention", Education Corner, https://www.educationcorner.com/bullying-facts-statistics-and-prevention.html

[106] Citizens Commission on Human Rights International, "Psychiatric Drugs: Create Violence & Suicide", March 2018, 15

[107] "School Shootings: Mental Health Watchdog Says Psychotropic Drug Use by School Shooters Merits Federal Investigation", February 21, 2018 https://www.prnewswire.com/news-releases/school-shootings-mental-health-watchdog-says-psychotropic-drug-use-by-school-shooters-merits-federal-investigation-300601826.html

[108] "Chapter IV MENTAL HEALTH HISTORY OF SEUNG HUI CHO", p33, https://powersoften.net/documents/cr/VirginiaTech/chapter4_mentalhealth.pdf

[109] Jessie Klein, "If Cho had not been bullied …", April 26, 2007 https://www.newsday.com/opinion/if-cho-had-not-been-bullied-1.573555

[110] "High school classmates say gunman was bullied", April 15, 2008 https://www.nbcnews.com/id/wbna18202709

[111] "Seung Hui Cho's "Manifesto"" https://schoolshooters.info/sites/default/files/cho_manifesto_1.1.pdf

[112] Reed Williams, "No drugs found in Cho's body", Jun 21, 2007 https://roanoke.com/archive/no-drugs-found-in-chos-body/article_26ac1869-5720-56f1-8c7b-2df44165b1be.html

[113] Salynn Boyles, "Paxil Warning for Depressed Kids", June 11, 2003 https://www.webmd.com/depression/news/20030611/paxil-warning-for-depressed-kids

[114] Carol A. Clark, "A Brief History of Psychotropic Drugs Prescribed to Mass Murderers", January 16, 2013 https://ladailypost.com/a-brief-history-of-psychotropic-drugs-prescribed-to-mass-murderers/

[115] https://www.accessdata.fda.gov/drugsatfda_docs/label/2011/018936s091lbl.pdf

[116] Dave Cullen, "The reluctant killer", April 24, 2009 https://www.theguardian.com/world/2009/apr/25/dave-cullen-columbine

[117] "Eric Harris" https://reallifevillains.miraheze.org/wiki/Eric_Harris

[118] C. Shepard, "Eric Harris' Journal", http://acolumbinesite.com/eric/writing/journal/journal.php

[119] Dave Cullen, "The Depressive and the Psychopath", Slate, April 20, 2004 https://slate.com/news-and-politics/2004/04/at-last-we-know-why-the-columbine-killers-did-it.html

[120] David Olinger, "Killer's parents to meet investigators", Denver Post, October 3, 1999 https://extras.denverpost.com/news/shot1003a.htm

[121] David Olinger, "Killer's parents to meet investigators", Denver Post, October 3, 1999 https://extras.denverpost.com/news/shot1003a.htm

[122] Howard Pankratz, "Columbine bullying no myth, panel told", Denver Post, October 3, 2000 https://extras.denverpost.com/news/col1003a.htm

[123] Howard Pankratz, "Columbine bullying no myth, panel told", Denver Post, October 3, 2000 https://extras.denverpost.com/news/col1003a.htm

[124] https://en.wikipedia.org/wiki/Columbine_High_School_massacre

[125] Greg Toppo, "10 years later, the real story behind Columbine", USA Today, https://usatoday30.usatoday.com/news/nation/2009-04-13-columbine-myths_N.htm

[126] Ann Schrader, "Drug found in Harris' body", https://extras.denverpost.com/news/shot0504e.htm

[127] Steve Salvatore, "Columbine shooter was prescribed anti-depressant", April 29, 1999 http://www.cnn.com/HEALTH/9904/29/luvox.explainer/

[128] Peter R. Breggin, M.D., "Eric Harris was taking Luvox (a Prozac-like drug) at the time of the Littleton murders", April 30, 1999 http://psychrights.org/stories/EricHarris.htm

[129] National Alliance On Mental Illness, "Fluvoxamine (Luvox)", https://www.nami.org/About-Mental-Illness/Treatments/Mental-Health-Medications/Types-of-Medication/Fluvoxamine-(Luvox)

[130] Andrew Solomon, "The Reckoning - The father of the Sandy Hook killer searches for answers." March 10, 2014 https://www.newyorker.com/magazine/2014/03/17/the-reckoning

[131] Andrew Solomon, "The Reckoning - The father of the Sandy Hook killer searches for answers." March 10, 2014 https://www.newyorker.com/magazine/2014/03/17/the-reckoning

[132] Pamela Engel, "New Details Revealed About Ryan Lanza's Interrogation After The Sandy Hook Massacre", Dec 7, 2013 https://www.businessinsider.com/ryan-lanzas-interrogation-in-matthew-lysiak-book-2013-12

[133] Ruth Marcus, "Nancy Lanza, a mother tragic and infuriating", November 26, 2013 https://www.washingtonpost.com/opinions/ruth-marcus-nancy-lanza-a-mother-tragic-and-infuriating/2013/11/26/30efee1c-56cb-11e3-835d-e7173847c7cc_story.html

[134] "Understanding sensory processing issues", https://www.understood.org/en/learning-thinking-differences/child-learning-disabilities/sensory-processing-issues/understanding-sensory-processing-issues?utm_source=google&utm_medium=paid&utm_campaign=evrgrn-may20-fm&gclid=Cj0KCQjw5PGFBhC2ARIsAlFIMNcY1dMF69-NG-YB5Yw6ykXqHYpfcbLcL0dEwYzvWnmKMZ07REX3CUcaAkEvEALw_wcB

[135] Alison Leigh Cowan, "'Completely Untreated' Before Newtown Shootings, Report Says", Nov. 21, 2014 https://www.nytimes.com/2014/11/22/nyregion/before-newtown-shootings-adam-lanzas-mental-problems-completely-untreated-report-says.html

[136] Alison Leigh Cowan, "'Completely Untreated' Before Newtown Shootings, Report Says", Nov. 21, 2014 https://www.nytimes.com/2014/11/22/nyregion/before-newtown-shootings-adam-lanzas-mental-problems-completely-untreated-report-says.html

[137] Andrew Solomon, "The Reckoning - The father of the Sandy Hook killer searches for answers." March 10, 2014 https://www.newyorker.com/magazine/2014/03/17/the-reckoning

[138] "Sandy Hook shootings: Four things revealed by FBI files", October 25, 2017 https://www.bbc.com/news/world-us-canada-41749336

[139] Alison Leigh Cowan, "Adam Lanza's Mental Problems 'Completely Untreated' Before Newtown Shootings, Report Says", Nov. 21, 2014 https://www.nytimes.com/2014/11/22/nyregion/before-newtown-shootings-adam-lanzas-mental-problems-completely-untreated-report-says.html

[140] "Unreported Information Showing Nikolas Cruz's Troubling Behavior ", http://www.fdle.state.fl.us/MSDHS/Meetings/November-Meeting-Documents/Nov-13-145pm-Cruz-Behavior-Chris-Lyons.aspx

[141] Michelle Mark , Kieran Corcoran , and David Choi, "This timeline shows exactly how the Parkland shooting unfolded", Feb 14, 2019 https://www.businessinsider.com/timeline-shows-how-the-parkland-florida-school-shooting-unfolded-2018-2

[142] Megan O'Matz, "Mental health provider had long history with Parkland shooter. Was agency negligent?", January 16, 2019 https://www.sun-sentinel.com/local/broward/parkland/florida-school-shooting/fl-ne-henderson-cruz-civil-suit-20190116-story.html

[143] Carol Marbin Miller and Nicholas Nehamas, "Nikolas Cruz's birth mom had a violent, criminal past. Could it help keep him off Death Row?", September, 5, 2018 https://www.miamiherald.com/news/local/community/broward/article216909390.html

[144] Brittany Wallman, Paula McMahon, Megan O'Matz and Susannah Bryan, "Lost, lonely Nikolas Cruz was 'school shooter in the making'", February 25, 2018 https://www.nydailynews.com/news/national/lost-lonely-nikolas-cruz-school-shooter-making-article-1.3840553

[145] Brittany Wallman, Paula McMahon, Megan O'Matz and Susannah Bryan, "Lost, lonely Nikolas Cruz was 'school shooter in the making'", February 25, 2018 https://www.nydailynews.com/news/national/lost-lonely-nikolas-cruz-school-shooter-making-article-1.3840553

146 "36 Shocking Statistics on Fatherless Homes", October 4, 2018, https://lifeisbeautiful.org/statistics-on-fatherless-homes/

147 Brittany Wallman, Paula McMahon, Megan O'Matz and Susannah Bryan, "Lost, lonely Nikolas Cruz was 'school shooter in the making'", February 25, 2018 https://www.nydailynews.com/news/national/lost-lonely-nikolas-cruz-school-shooter-making-article-1.3840553

148 Sabrina Lolo, Al Pefley, "Parkland school shooter Nikolas Cruz's confession released", August 6th 2018 https://cbs12.com/news/local/parkland-school-shooter-nikolas-cruzs-confession-released

149 Brittany Wallman, Paula McMahon, Megan O'Matz and Susannah Bryan, "Lost, lonely Nikolas Cruz was 'school shooter in the making'", February 25, 2018 https://www.nydailynews.com/news/national/lost-lonely-nikolas-cruz-school-shooter-making-article-1.3840553

150 Amy Morin, LCSW, "Bullying Statistics Everyone Should Know", Very Well Family, April 19, 2019 https://www.verywellfamily.com/bullying-statistics-to-know-4589438

151 Lucas Daprile, "Florida school shooting: Student knew Cruz: 'I could have said something to administrators'", February 15, 2018 https://www.tcpalm.com/story/news/2018/02/15/florida-school-shooting-student-could-have-said-something-administrators/341707002/

152 Megan O'Matz, "School shooter tormented his mother yet she escorted him to buy an AK-47", October 19, 2018 https://www.sun-sentinel.com/local/broward/parkland/florida-school-shooting/fl-ne-cruz-ak-47-story.html

153 "Unreported Information Showing Nikolas Cruz's Troubling Behavior ", http://www.fdle.state.fl.us/MSDHS/Meetings/November-Meeting-Documents/Nov-13-145pm-Cruz-Behavior-Chris-Lyons.aspx

[154] "Unreported Information Showing Nikolas Cruz's Troubling Behavior ", http://www.fdle.state.fl.us/MSDHS/Meetings/November-Meeting-Documents/Nov-13-145pm-Cruz-Behavior-Chris-Lyons.aspx

[155] Natalie Musumeci, "Parkland shooter was searched for weapons every morning before school", July 26, 2019 https://nypost.com/2019/07/26/parkland-shooter-was-searched-for-weapons-every-morning-before-school/

[156] Natalie Musumeci, "Parkland shooter was searched for weapons every morning before school", July 26, 2019 https://nypost.com/2019/07/26/parkland-shooter-was-searched-for-weapons-every-morning-before-school/

[157] Jessica Bakeman, "Backlash Follows Revelations That Parkland Shooter Was Referred To PROMISE Program", May 7, 2018 https://www.wlrn.org/news/2018-05-07/backlash-follows-revelations-that-parkland-shooter-was-referred-to-promise-program

[158] Colin Dwyer, "Texas Church Shooter May Have Been Motivated To Kill By 'Domestic Situation'", November 6, 2017 https://www.npr.org/sections/thetwo-way/2017/11/06/562299408/texas-church-shooter-may-have-been-motivated-to-kill-by-domestic-situation

[159] Jennifer Dzikowski, "Devin Patrick Kelley's Family: 5 Fast Facts You Need to Know", November 8, 2017 https://heavy.com/news/2017/11/devin-patrick-kelley-family-wife-danielle-shields-facebook/

[160] Rory Tingle, "REVEALED: Texas church shooter had cannabis and prescription drugs in his system when he killed 26 members of a congregation before shooting himself in the head" June 29, 2018 https://www.dailymail.co.uk/news/article-5900683/Autopsy-confirms-Texas-church-gunman-died-suicide.html

[161] Emily Shugerman, "'He had a Columbine feel to him': Former classmates recall Texas shooting suspect Devin Kelley", November 7, 2017 https://www.independent.co.uk/news/world/americas/devin-kelley-texas-shooting-new-braunfels-high-school-columbine-a8041926.html

[162] Jacob Gershman and Nancy A. Youssef, "Texas Church Shooter Was Ticking Time Bomb", May 7, 2018 https://www.wsj.com/articles/texas-church-shooter-burst-with-violent-rage-1525685401

[163] Melinda Smith, M.A., Lawrence Robinson, and Jeanne Segal, Ph.D. Reviewed by Anna Glezer, M.D., "Anxiety Medication", July 2021 https://www.helpguide.org/articles/anxiety/anxiety-medication.htm#

[164] Eli Rosenberg, "Texas gunman's ex-wife said he once put a gun to her head and asked, 'Do you want to die?'", November 12, 2017 https://www.washingtonpost.com/news/post-nation/wp/2017/11/12/texas-gunmans-ex-wife-said-he-once-put-a-gun-to-her-head-and-asked-do-you-want-to-die/

[165] Emily Shugerman, "'He had a Columbine feel to him': Former classmates recall Texas shooting suspect Devin Kelley", November 7, 2017 https://www.independent.co.uk/news/world/americas/devin-kelley-texas-shooting-new-braunfels-high-school-columbine-a8041926.html

[166] Tracy Connor; Daniel Arkin. "Texas Gunman Devin Kelley Escaped from Mental Health Facility in 2012". NBC News.November 7, 2017 https://www.nbcnews.com/storyline/texas-church-shooting/texas-gunman-devin-kelley-escaped-mental-health-facility-2012-n818496

[167] Eli Rosenberg, "Texas gunman's ex-wife said he once put a gun to her head and asked, 'Do you want to die?'", November 12, 2017 https://www.washingtonpost.com/news/post-nation/wp/2017/11/12/texas-gunmans-ex-wife-said-he-once-put-a-gun-to-her-head-and-asked-do-you-want-to-die/

[168] Associated Press, "Texas gunman had history of violence years before shooting", August 26, 2020 https://apnews.com/article/shootings-tx-state-wire-us-news-religion-96f3275c99658ddbcacf4b65b224f5e2

[169] Emanuella Grinberg and Eliott C. McLaughlin, "Texas church shooter Devin Patrick Kelley's troubled past emerges", November 8, 2017 https://www.cnn.com/2017/11/06/us/devin-kelley-texas-church-shooting-suspect/index.html

[170] Tom Vsnden Brook, "Air Force failed four times to prevent Sutherland Springs church killer from buying guns", December 7, 2018 https://www.usatoday.com/story/news/politics/2018/12/07/air-force-failed-four-times-prevent-sutherland-springs-shooter-gun-purchase/2237400002/

[171] https://storage.courtlistener.com/recap/gov.uscourts.txwd.949434/gov.uscourts.txwd.949434.249.0_1.pdf

[172] Associated Press, "Texas gunman had history of violence years before shooting", August 26, 2020 https://apnews.com/article/shootings-tx-state-wire-us-news-religion-96f3275c99658ddbcacf4b65b224f5e2

[173] "Classmate: Batman killing spree suspect spent childhood in Castroville", July 23, 2012 https://www.ksbw.com/article/classmate-batman-killing-spree-suspect-spent-childhood-in-castroville/1049945

[174] Maria La Ganga, "What will Dr. Lynne Fenton say about her former patient James Holmes?", June 14, 2015 https://www.baltimoresun.com/la-na-dr-lynne-fenton-james-holmes-20150603-story.html

[175] Bernie Woodall, "Mateen altered looks, researched anti-psychotic drugs before attack", June 22, 2016 https://www.reuters.com/article/us-florida-shooting-mateen/mateen-altered-looks-researched-anti-psychotic-drugs-before-attack-idUSKCN0Z82LH

[176] Ed Pilkington and Jessica Elgot, "Orlando gunman Omar Mateen 'was a regular at Pulse nightclub'", June 14, 2016 https://www.theguardian.com/us-news/2016/jun/14/orlando-shooter-omar-mateen-was-a-regular-at-nightclub

[177] Ed Pilkington and Jessica Elgot, "Orlando gunman Omar Mateen 'was a regular at Pulse nightclub'", June 14, 2016 https://www.theguardian.com/us-news/2016/jun/14/orlando-shooter-omar-mateen-was-a-regular-at-nightclub

[178] Ayaan Hirsi Ali, "Islam's Jihad Against Homosexuals", June 13, 2016 https://www.wsj.com/articles/islams-jihad-against-homosexuals-1465859170

[179] Tucker Reals, "What has the Orlando gunman's father said?", June 13, 2016 https://www.cbsnews.com/news/orlando-shooting-omar-mateen-father-seddique-mateen-taliban-god-punish-gays/

[180] Merrit Kennedy, "Investigators Say Orlando Shooter Showed Few Warning Signs Of Radicalization", June 18, 2016 https://www.npr.org/sections/thetwo-way/2016/06/18/482621690/investigators-say-orlando-shooter-showed-few-warning-signs-of-radicalization

[181] Becton Loveless, "Bullying Epidemic: Facts, Statistics and Prevention", Education Corner, https://www.educationcorner.com/bullying-facts-statistics-and-prevention.html

[182] Palm Beach Post Staff, "Omar Mateen used steroids for years, didn't have HIV autopsy finds", July 16, 2016 https://www.palmbeachpost.com/news/omar-mateen-used-steroids-for-years-didn-have-hiv-autopsy-finds/b2tXlB58VaVhfElLg3V0XK/

[183] Del Quentin Wilber, "Autopsy: Fla. shooter likely longtime steroid user", https://digitaledition.baltimoresun.com/tribune/article_popover.aspx?guid=0c77bfd2-1192-453d-a010-91fe62b0ca8e

[184] MedicineNet, "Predinsone Side Effects and Adverse Effects", October 18, 2019 https://www.medicinenet.com/side_effects_and_adverse_effects_of_prednisone/article.htm#what_is_prednisone_how_does_it_work

[185] "LVMPD Criminal Investigative Report of the 1 October Mass Casualty Shooting", https://www.lvmpd.com/en-us/Documents/1-October-FIT-Criminal-Investigative-Report-FINAL_080318.pdf

[186] Emanuella Grinberg, "Something went 'incredibly wrong' with Las Vegas gunman, brother says", October 6, 2017 https://edition.cnn.com/2017/10/02/us/las-vegas-attack-stephen-paddock-trnd/index.html

[187] "Las Vegas shooter Stephen Paddock was born in Clinton", October 6, 2017 https://www.desmoinesregister.com/story/news/2017/10/06/las-vegas-shooter-stephen-paddock-born-clinton/729109001/

[188] Paul Harasim, "Las Vegas Strip shooter prescribed anti-anxiety drug in June", October 3, 2017 https://www.reviewjournal.com/local/the-strip/las-vegas-strip-shooter-prescribed-anti-anxiety-drug-in-june/

[189] Northern Illinois University, "Report of the February 14, 2008 Shootings at Northern Illinois University", https://www.niu.edu/forward/_pdfs/archives/feb14report.pdf

[190] Jodi S. Cohen and Stacy St. Clair, "Father says shooting motives a mystery", April 20, 2008 https://www.chicagotribune.com/news/ct-xpm-2008-04-20-chi-080420niu-shootings-father-story.html

[191] Eddy Montville, "NIU gunman's essays reveal his alienation", April 19, 2008 https://www.rrstar.com/article/20080419/NEWS/304199910

[192] Abbie Boudreau and Scott Zamost, "Girlfriend: Shooter was taking cocktail of 3 drugs", CNN, https://www.cnn.com/2008/CRIME/02/20/shooter.girlfriend/index.html

[193] Jayne Leonard, "What to know about fluoxetine withdrawal:, April 28, 2021 https://www.medicalnewstoday.com/articles/fluoxetine-withdrawal

[194] David J. Krajicek, "Mass Killers: Inside The Minds Of Men Who Murder", 50-51

[195] Arjun Chanmugam, Patrick Triplett, Gabor Kelen, "Emergency Psychiatry", 28

[196] David J. Krajicek, "Mass Killers: Inside The Minds Of Men Who Murder", 36

[197] Terry Moran, "Inside Cho's Mind", August 30, 2007 https://abcnews.go.com/Nightline/Story?id=3541157&page=2

[198] David J. Krajicek, "Mass Killers: Inside The Minds Of Men Who Murder", 35

[199] David J. Krajicek, "Mass Killers: Inside The Minds Of Men Who Murder", 36

[200] Terry Moran, "Inside Cho's Mind", August 30, 2007 https://abcnews.go.com/Nightline/Story?id=3541157&page=2

[201] Moira Colley, "PETA Statement: Suspected High School Shooter Has Reported History of Animal Abuse", February 15, 2018 https://www.peta.org/media/news-releases/peta-statement-suspected-high-school-shooter-reported-history-animal-abuse/

[202] Megan O'Matz, "School shooter tormented his mother yet she escorted him to buy an AK-47", October 19, 2018 https://www.sun-sentinel.com/local/broward/parkland/florida-school-shooting/fl-ne-cruz-ak-47-story.html

[203] Kristin Hugo, "Texas Church Shooter Devin Kelley Was Charged With Animal Cruelty After Beating a Dog With His Fists", November 7, 2017 https://www.newsweek.com/texas-church-shooter-devin-kelley-was-charged-animal-cruelty-after-beating-dog-703960

[204] "Who was Texas church gunman Devin Patrick Kelley?", November 7, 2017 https://www.bbc.com/news/world-us-canada-41884342

[205] David J. Krajicek, "Mass Killers: Inside The Minds Of Men Who Murder", 36

[206] Meg Kelly, "Do 98 percent of mass public shootings happen in gun free zones?", May 10, 2018 https://www.journalgazette.net/news/fact-check/20180510/do-98-percent-of-mass-public-shootings-happen-in-gun-free-zones

[207] Meg Kelly, "Do 98 percent of mass public shootings happen in gun free zones?", May 10, 2018 https://www.journalgazette.net/news/fact-check/20180510/do-98-percent-of-mass-public-shootings-happen-in-gun-free-zones

[208] "Federally Banned Locations for Carrying Firearms" https://www.usconcealedcarry.com/resources/federal-ccw-law/federally-banned-locations-for-carrying-firearms/

[209] Centers for Disease Control and Prevention, "Preventing Bullying", https://www.cdc.gov/violenceprevention/youthviolence/bullyingresearch/fastfact.html

[210] American Psychological Association, "Bullying", https://www.apa.org/topics/bullying

[211] US Secret Service and US Department of Education, The Final Report and Findings of the Safe School Initiative and Implications of School Attacks in the United States. May 2002, p.34.

[212] https://safe2tell.org/history

[213] https://safe2tell.org/history

[214] T.J. Mathews, M.S.; and Brady E. Hamilton, Ph.D., "Mean Age of Mothers is on the Rise: United States, 2000–2014", 2016 https://www.cdc.gov/nchs/products/databriefs/db232.htm

[215] James Pethokoukis, "Julia's mother: Why a single mom is better off with a $29,000 job and welfare than taking a $69,000 job", July 12, 2012 https://www.aei.org/pethokoukis/julias-mother-why-a-single-mom-is-better-off-with-a-29000-job-and-welfare-than-taking-a-69000-job/

[216] Chris Edwards, "Capitol Police Funding", January 7, 2021 https://www.cato.org/blog/capitol-police-funding

[217] Chris Edwards, "Capitol Police Funding", January 7, 2021 https://www.cato.org/blog/capitol-police-funding

[218] Tim Walker, "'School Hardening' not making students safer, say experts", February 14, 2019 https://educationvotes.nea.org/2019/02/14/school-hardening-not-making-students-safer-say-experts/

[219] Lauren Camera, "Educators Endorse Safety Measures – Not Arming Teachers", February 11, 2019 https://www.usnews.com/news/education-news/articles/2019-02-11/educators-endorse-safety-measures-not-arming-teachers

[220] Tim Walker, "'School Hardening' Not Making Students Safer, Say Experts", February 14, 2019 https://www.nea.org/advocating-for-change/new-from-nea/school-hardening-not-making-students-safer-say-experts

[221] "Schenck v. United States, 249 U.S. 47 (1919)" https://supreme.justia.com/cases/federal/us/249/47/

[222] "Schenck v. United States, 249 U.S. 47 (1919)" https://supreme.justia.com/cases/federal/us/249/47/

[223] "Schenck v. United States, 249 U.S. 47 (1919)" https://supreme.justia.com/cases/federal/us/249/47/

[224] Brian Schwartz, "Bloomberg's huge donation helps his gun safety group raise record revenue in 2018", CNBC, November 26, 2019 https://www.cnbc.com/2019/11/26/bloomberg-vs-nra-huge-donation-lifts-gun-safety-groups-revenue.html

225 "Guns & Ammunition Manufacturing in the US - Employment Statistics 2005–2027", April 29, 2021 https:// www.ibisworld.com/industry-statistics/employment/guns-ammunition-manufacturing-united-states/

226 "Guns & Ammunition Manufacturing in the US - Employment Statistics 2005–2027", April 29, 2021 https:// www.ibisworld.com/industry-statistics/employment/guns-ammunition-manufacturing-united-states/

227 Brian Schwartz, "Bloomberg's huge donation helps his gun safety group raise record revenue in 2018", CNBC, November 26, 2019 https://www.cnbc.com/2019/11/26/bloomberg-vs-nra-huge-donation-lifts-gun-safety-groups-revenue.html

228 Priyanka Boghani, "How Gun Control Groups Are Closing the Spending Gap with the NRA", March 24, 2020 https:// www.pbs.org/wgbh/frontline/article/how-gun-control-groups-are-closing-the-spending-gap-with-the-nra/

229 Priyanka Boghani, "How Gun Control Groups Are Closing the Spending Gap with the NRA", March 24, 2020 https:// www.pbs.org/wgbh/frontline/article/how-gun-control-groups-are-closing-the-spending-gap-with-the-nra/

230 Mason Walker, "U.S. newsroom employment has fallen 26% since 2008", July 13, 2021 https://www.pewresearch.org/fact-tank/2021/07/13/u-s-newsroom-employment-has-fallen-26-since-2008/

231 Brad Adgate, "As Their Ratings Drop, TV Networks Fault Nielsen. Media Researchers Weigh In", April 20, 2021 https:// www.forbes.com/sites/bradadgate/2021/04/20/as-ratings-drop-tv-networks-fault-nielsen-media-researchers-weigh-in/? sh=3bb259462ee1

232 Rick Porter, "TV Long View: Five Years of Network Ratings Declines in Context:, September 21, 2019 https:// www.hollywoodreporter.com/tv/tv-news/five-years-network-ratings-declines-explained-1241524/

[233] Mira Rakicevic, "21 Captivating Reading Statistics and Facts for 2021", February 23, 2021 https://comfyliving.net/reading-statistics/

[234] Tanner Stening, "There's No Epidemic Of Mass Shootings. There Is An Epidemic Of Fear", June 30, 2021 https://news.northeastern.edu/2021/06/30/the-myths-and-the-realities-of-mass-shootings-in-the-us-today/

[235] Tanner Stening, "There's No Epidemic Of Mass Shootings. There Is An Epidemic Of Fear", June 30, 2021 https://news.northeastern.edu/2021/06/30/the-myths-and-the-realities-of-mass-shootings-in-the-us-today/

[236] Priyanka Boghani, "How Gun Control Groups Are Closing the Spending Gap with the NRA", March 24, 2020 https://www.pbs.org/wgbh/frontline/article/how-gun-control-groups-are-closing-the-spending-gap-with-the-nra/

[237] OpenSecrets.org, https://www.opensecrets.org/outside-spending/spenders-industries?cycle=2020

[238] "Real Median Personal Income in the United States" https://fred.stlouisfed.org/series/MEPAINUSA672N

[239] OpenSecrets.org, "Gun Control" https://www.opensecrets.org/industries/summary.php?ind=Q12&cycle=2020&recipdetail=M&sortorder=U

[240] Dr Cheryl Barton, "Annual revenue of top 10 big pharma companies", March 3, 2020 https://www.thepharmaletter.com/article/annual-revenue-of-top-10-big-pharma-companies

[241] Aimee Picchi, "Big Pharma ushers in new year by raising prices of more than 1,000 drugs," CBS News, January 2, 2019, available at https://www.cbsnews.com/news/drug-prices-oxycontin-predaxa-purdue-pharmaceuticals-boehringer-ingelheim/.

242 Marc Bekoff Ph.D., "We're Being Bombarded by Ads for Drugs", October 20, 2019 https://www.psychologytoday.com/us/blog/animal-emotions/201910/were-being-bombarded-ads-drugs

243 Marc Bekoff Ph.D., "We're Being Bombarded by Ads for Drugs", October 20, 2019 https://www.psychologytoday.com/us/blog/animal-emotions/201910/were-being-bombarded-ads-drugs

244 Julia Stoll, "Number of TV households in the United States from season 2000-2001 to season 2020-2021", July 13, 2021 https://www.statista.com/statistics/243789/number-of-tv-households-in-the-us/

245 Jeremy Hobson, "After Parkland, Don't 'Turn Our Schools Into Prisons,' Says Education Activist", March 07, 2018 https://www.wbur.org/hereandnow/2018/03/07/school-shootings-security

246 Jeremy Hobson, "After Parkland, Don't 'Turn Our Schools Into Prisons,' Says Education Activist", March 07, 2018 https://www.wbur.org/hereandnow/2018/03/07/school-shootings-security

247 Jeremy Hobson, "After Parkland, Don't 'Turn Our Schools Into Prisons,' Says Education Activist", March 07, 2018 https://www.wbur.org/hereandnow/2018/03/07/school-shootings-security

248 Jennifer Garrett, "How Members of Congress Practice School Choice", June 13, 2000 https://www.heritage.org/education/report/how-members-congress-practice-school-choice-0#pgfId=1083971

249 Jennifer Garrett, "How Members of Congress Practice School Choice", June 13, 2000 https://www.heritage.org/education/report/how-members-congress-practice-school-choice-0#pgfId=1083971

[250] Chicago Tribune, "Tracking Chicago shooting victims: 2,021 so far this year, 164 more than in 2020", July 7, 2021 https://www.chicagotribune.com/data/ct-shooting-victims-map-charts-htmlstory.html

[251] Skoolboy, "Where Will Malia Ann and Sasha Obama Go to School?", November 07, 2008 https://www.edweek.org/policy-politics/opinion-where-will-malia-ann-and-sasha-obama-go-to-school/2008/11

[252] Statista, "Number of mass shootings in the United States between 1982 and May 2021, by shooter's gender", May 2021 https://www.statista.com/statistics/476445/mass-shootings-in-the-us-by-shooter-s-gender/

[253] Mark Meckler, "Of The 27 Deadliest Mass Shooters, 26 Of Them Had One Thing In Common", February 20, 2018 https://www.patheos.com/blogs/markmeckler/2018/02/27-deadliest-mass-shooters-26-one-thing-common/

[254] National Fatherhood Initiative, "The Proof Is In: Father Absence Harms Children", https://www.fatherhood.org/father-absence-statistic

Hot Sauce & Seasonings

| ButthurtBrand.com |